The Garden Lover's Guide to the Midwest

PRINCETON ARCHITECTURAL PRESS   NEW YORK

PAUL BENNETT

The Garden Lover's Guide
to the Midwest

Princeton Architectural Press
37 East 7th Street
New York, NY 10003
212.995.9620

For a free catalog of other books published by Princeton Architectural
Press, call toll free 1.800.722.6657 or visit www.papress.com

EDITING: Jan Cigliano
DESIGN: Sara E. Stemen
LAYOUT: Adam B. Bohannon
MAPS: Jane Garvie
Special thanks to Ann Alter, Eugenia Bell, Caroline Green, Beth Harrison,
Mia Ihara, Clare Jacobson, Leslie Ann Kent, Mark Lamster, Anne Nitschke,
Lottchen Shivers, Jennifer Thompson, and Deb Wood of Princeton
Architectural Press

—Kevin C. Lippert, *publisher*

Library of Congress Cataloguing-in-Publication Data
Bennett, Paul, 1970–
    Garden lover's guide to the Midwest / by Paul Bennett
        p. cm.
    Includes bibliographical references (p. 125) and index.
    ISBN 1–56898–165–1 (alk. paper)
    1. Gardens—Middle West—Guidebooks. 2. Middle West—
    Guidebooks. I. Title.
SB466.U65 M532 2000
712'.0977—dc21   99–050000
                                          CIP

PHOTOS: *Cover,* Minnesota Landscape Arboretum; *title page,* Dow Gardens,
Michigan; *page ii,* Frederick Meijer Gaden, Michigan; *page iii,* Dawes
Arboretum, Ohio

PRINTED AND BOUND IN HONG KONG
04 03 02 01 00   5 4 3 2 1
FIRST EDITION

Contents

How to use this book

This guide is written for travelers who wish to visit the most historic and beautiful gardens in the midwestern United States, from the prairie style gardens of Illinois and Michigan, to the kitchen gardens of Kansas, and the botanical teaching gardens of Minnesota and Oklahoma.

The book is divided into five chapters covering the major states of the Midwest. Each chapter comprises an introductory section with a regional map and a list of the gardens, followed by entries on each garden. The numbers found on the regional maps can be used to locate the numbered entries within the chapters. These entries are accompanied by detailed at-a-glance information telling the reader about the garden's main characteristics and nearby sights of interest. The guide also includes five major gardens, beautifully illustrated with three-dimensional plans.

GREAT LAKES WEST REGION:

Illinois, Indiana

As many gardeners might suppose, Chicago dominates the garden scene in this part of the Midwest. It is a major city with the public and private infrastructure to support a number of important gardens. The Chicago Botanic Garden, located on the lake shore north of the city, is the most prominent. With 385 acres of formal and landscape gardens, it is the largest garden in the area; yet at just thirty years old it is also one of the newest. Within the city of Chicago and its immediate suburbs are three important historic conservatories. Jens Jensen, a Danish-born landscape architect whose "prairie style" revolutionized gardening in Chicago, designed Garfield Conservatory on the west side in the 1910s. Filled with lush tapestry of tropical plants, the conservatory amazed residents of this cold, northern metropolis with its exotic array. Thanks to its success, the Lincoln Park and Oak Park Conservatories followed shortly thereafter. Each building is relatively small when compared with contemporary domes and glasshouses, and objectively the architecture of each is quite uninspired. Yet these are some of the most intimate and forgotten spaces in the city, each of which has been artfully designed by either a skilled landscape architect (Jensen) or a knowledgeable gardener imitating his influential lead.

As the population and geography of Chicago grew exponentially in the first decades of this century, great estates arose on its outskirts. Today, two of these are home to wonderful gardens. One, the Morton Arboretum, is a large academic institution containing a world-renowned collection of trees on what was once the

OPPOSITE: *A gentle opening creates a subtle space at Cantigny in Wheaton, Illinois.*

19

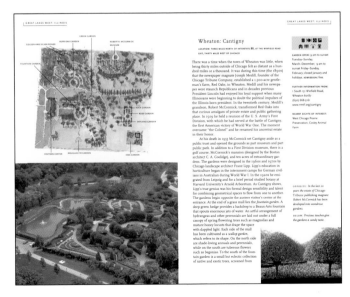

Wheaton: Cantigny

LOCATION: THREE MILES NORTH OF INTERSTATE 88, AT THE WINFIELD ROAD EXIT, THIRTY MILES WEST OF CHICAGO

There was a time when the town of Wheaton was little, when being thirty miles outside of Chicago felt as distant as a hundred miles or a thousand. It was during this time (the 1890s) that the newspaper magnate Joseph Medill, founder of the Chicago Tribune Company, established a 1,500-acre gentleman's farm, Red Oaks, in Wheaton. Medill and his newspaper were staunch Republicans and in decades previous President Lincoln had enjoyed his loyal support when many Illinoisans were beginning to doubt the political impulses of the Illinois-born president. In the twentieth century, Medill's grandson, Robert McCormick, transformed Red Oaks into that curious amalgam of private estate and public gathering place. In 1919 he held a reunion of the U. S. Army's First Division, with which he had served at the battle of Cantigny, the first American victory of World War One. The moment overcame "the Colonel" and he renamed his ancestral estate in their honor.

At his death in 1955 McCormick set Cantigny aside as a public trust and opened the grounds as part museum and part public park. In addition to a First Division museum, there is a golf course. McCormick's mansion (designed by the Boston architect C. A. Coolidge), and ten acres of extraordinary gardens. The gardens were designed in the 1960s and 1970s by Chicago landscape architect Franz Lipp. Lipp's education in horticulture began in the internment camps for German civilians in Australian during World War I. In the 1920s he emigrated from Leipzig and for a brief period studied botany at Harvard University's Arnold Arboretum. As Cantigny shows, Lipp's true genius was his formal design sensibility and talent for combining geometrical spaces to flow from one to another. The gardens begin opposite the austere visitor's center at the entrance. At the end of a grass mall lies the fountain garden. A deep green hedge provides a backdrop to a Beaux-Arts fountain that spouts enormous jets of water. An artful arrangement of hydrangeas and other perennials are laid out under a full canopy of spring flowering trees such as magnolias and mature honey locusts that drape the space with dappled light. Each side of the mall has been cultivated as a scallop garden, which refers to its shape. On the north side are shade-loving annuals and perennials, while on the south are tuberous flowers such as begonias. To the south of the fountain garden is a small but eclectic collection of native and exotic trees, screened from

GARDEN OPEN: 9 am to sunset Tuesday–Sunday, March–December; 9 am to sunset Friday–Sunday, February; closed January and holidays. ADMISSION: free.

FURTHER INFORMATION FROM:
1 South 151 Winfield Road, Wheaton 60187
(630) 668-5161
www.rrmtf.org/cantigny

NEARBY SIGHTS OF INTEREST:
West Chicago Prairie Preservation; Cosley Animal Farm

OPPOSITE: *In the last 20 years the estate of Chicago Tribune publishing magnate Robert McCormick has been developed into wondrous gardens.*

BELOW: *Precious touches give the gardens a candy taste.*

Foreword

Touring the Midwest in search of gardens is educational, in part because the entire region can be considered one vast kitchen garden. Roaming through Indiana, Illinois, and Iowa the landscape becomes engulfed by fields of crops, as far as the eye can see. In one place you will see wheat, in another corn, and soybeans farther along. The variation, on a large scale, is as dynamic as any botanic garden. If an ardent gardener admits that truly his work is only to oversee the magic of nature, then the farmer or agribusinessman feel this even more strongly. It is a flighty business, dependent on a kind of voodoo—just like a garden.

It is strange, then, that within this uniquely gardenesque landscape, of which there are few equals the world over, garden design has not taken a cue from agriculture. There are a few exceptions. At the agricultural universities there has been an effort over the years to educate the public about agricultural gardening, particularly in the realm of organic gardening. But the majority of the gardens in this region either ignore or make outright efforts to counteract the agricultural heritage of their region. There can be little doubt about the validity of this second point. Mass farming has had a tremendous impact and altered the Midwest landscape over the last one hundred years, more than any amount of city building or industrial activity. When the first pioneer farmers came to Ohio, then Indiana, and the Great Plains beyond, they found verdant, wild prairie lands, intermingled with woodlands. In just two hundred years, much of that landscape is gone, turned under by the plow. In the last decade, impelled no doubt by increasing awareness of ecology, there has been a much-needed effort to preserve and replant prairie landscapes all across the region. Nowadays, most good public gardens either have a prairie garden or are building one. And enthusiasm for the cause only grows.

History tells a story, and we can read from this certain lessons. Surely bad things happen, and it is never questionable to redress old mistakes in order to make a better future. This is undoubtedly true when we speak of the environment, in which the mistakes we make can have life-threatening consequences. And yet it's probably to our detriment to cast out certain legacies, especially when those legacies are fundamental to who we are. This is the case with the Midwest agricultural landscape, which is under assault on all fronts—from sprawling suburban communities, overuse of chemical fertilizers, to imported produce. While it is not happening yet, one cannot help but wonder that in twenty or thirty years Midwest gardens, in addition to their display of Victorian exotics and native plants, will also include an American farm garden. By then it may just be a quaint throwback, a museum piece to remember bygone times.

Introduction

Most people do not think of the Midwest as a place for gardens. The weather is harsh, with cold temperatures, high winds, and plenty of snow. But just as the saying states, "what doesn't kill you makes you stronger," these pressures have helped to cultivate a rich, if hardy, gardening culture in this region.

The story begins in the final decades of the nineteenth century, when midwestern cities were just beginning to grow into sizable urban areas, acquiring wealth, and turning toward true city-building: the making of such public institutions as art museums, libraries, and parks. Working from the example of European cities and their progeny in the eastern United States, midwestern cities such as Chicago, St. Louis, and Cincinnati also built major botanical gardens. Because of climatic pressures, most of these gardens were enclosed in conservatories, and during the 1890s and 1900s the New York-based Lord and Burnham company was busy throughout the Midwest erecting opulent glasshouses.

Botanical gardens first came about in England in the eighteenth and nineteenth centuries as British society became more democratic and public museums and libraries began to be built. Botanical gardens were a part of this movement, and the pinnacle, reached in the early nineteenth century, was the Royal Botanic Garden at Kew, which under the tutelage of Sir William Hooker became the world's leading research institution. Kew's plantsmen combed the world for exotic flora, which was put on display for all of England in the large conservatory built on the grounds in 1849. Kew strongly influenced the development in America of rival institutions, including the New York Botanical Garden, the Brooklyn Botanic Garden, and Boston's Arnold Arboretum. Long before any of these places came on the scene, however, there was the Missouri Botanical Garden, established in 1859, which has remained an undeniably potent force in the gardening world of the Midwest ever since.

Although Missouri has always been a major research institution, most of the botanical gardens scattered across the Midwest—and it is impressive to see them in such towns as Dubuque, Iowa and Toledo, Ohio—are not focused on science. Rather it is the idea of the public garden as a symbol of democracy that took fire in the Midwest during the early part of the twentieth century. Here, the genesis of Kew—the idea that gardens must be made available to masses—was taken to a truly populist level.

As a result of the interest in conservatories, what might be called the most typical Midwest garden, at least thirty years ago, was ironically a collection of palms, cycads, and other tropical rainforest plants. And if one lived in Chicago in the 1920s, you were more likely to be familiar with the exotic bromeliads just

Traditional mixed borders are just one part of a rich mixture of gardens that comprise the Chicago Botanic Garden in Glencoe, Illinois.

The spirit of Chicago Tribune publishing magnate Colonel Robert McCormick still emanates across the landscape of Cantigny in Wheaton, Illinois.

acquired by the Lincoln Park Conservatory than the native trees in northern Illinois region. All this began to change in the 1920s with a young Danish immigrant named Jens Jensen. Jensen was a horticulturist and landscape architect who became a park commissioner in Chicago. While his American contemporaries in landscape design were engrossed in the Beaux-Arts idiom or mimicking the Olmsted company's English landscape style, Jensen turned his attention to the landscape of Chicago, the prairie that even then was rapidly disappearing.

Jensen designed in what has come to be called the prairie style. Although he employed a few hardscape features, such as the distinctive "council ring" of stones that provides a place to rest and socialize in a garden, his designs were mostly informal, naturalistic prairie woodlands. Most people think of Jensen as a plant person because he championed a native palette, and anytime we see hawthorns or prairie grasses we tend to immediately think of him. But Jensen was interested in the entire landscape of the prairie, including the way that open space and woodlands interrelated, how gentle hills worked with small lakes, and how seasonal color could be used in subtle ways. The one conservatory that Jensen designed, the Garfield Conservatory in Chicago, is a remarkable combination of standard plant materials (meaning tropicals) in a flowing, natural, midwestern style. Although this has now become popular and given the label "immersion experience" in zoo and botanical garden design, Jensen believed it to be just a more beautiful and truer way to make landscapes.

Ossian Cole (O. C.) Simonds was a contemporary of Jensen, and perhaps played a more crucial role in propagating the prairie style in that parks and gardens across the Midwest frequently hired him to design. Simonds' work, although plentiful and good, was not as remarkable as Jensen's. He was a professional, and his work responded as much to his own dictates as that of his clients—as we see at the estate of Brucemore in Cedar Rapids, Iowa, and the Olbrich Botanical Gardens in Madison, Wisconsin.

Although it has been with us for almost a century, the prairie style is only now being rediscovered. Growing out of the environmental awareness born in the 1970s, strong interest in preserving local environments has taken hold in many communities. In the Midwest this energy is being directed toward designing and maintaining natural prairie landscapes. Much of this work is occurring on a large scale as nature preserves, while on the garden level naturalistic prairie gardens are appearing at most botanical gardens. There are a few of these, such as the prairie garden at the Chicago Botanic Garden,

ABOVE : *Influential landscape architect Jens Jensen designed many of the historic gardens around Chicago.*

BELOW: *Percival Gallagher's gardens at Oldfields (now the Indianapolis Museum of Art) are considered by many to be the most important in the country.*

designed by John Simonds in the 1960s, that are now old enough to be fully appreciated. But for the most part, this trend is just now picking up speed, and with a fervor.

Midwest gardeners and gardens have spent the second half of the twentieth century trying to find themselves. In some instances it looked as if the trends of Europe and the east coast were taking root. We find a few familiar estate gardens, with Italianate accents or an English landscape garden, here and there—born from certain booms in iron, or agribusiness, or chemicals. But these are scattered about, and surely not as prolific as might be expected. Then we see the botanical garden, probably the single most common garden type in the region. But these are expensive and require a great deal of municipal attention; and although there are several new ones planned in the region in the future, not every town wants one. Land preservation and the development of native prairies is a hot topic, giving rise to all sorts of conflicts between impassioned "nativists" and old fashioned botanical sorts, who ever praise the beauty of a whole host of invasives. As gardens evolve, they inevitably deal with this motley history. As a Midwest garden, what am I? Each must ask itself. Some answer right away with something that, at least for the moment, is certain. But most sway and rock with the tide, fluid to new developments in things as mundane as pest management or the next new annual hybrid, or as fundamental as how best to educate the local population about the beauty and significance of their world.

A tour through this region is delightfully diverse. Certain themes may seem to arise, while others will fall away. It takes a long time to see them all. Happy travels.

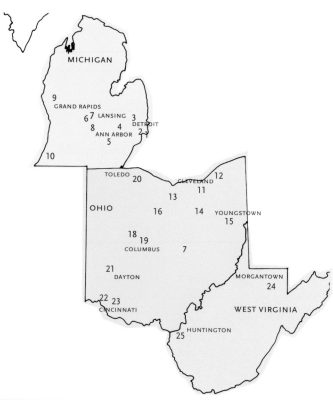

MICHIGAN

9 GRAND RAPIDS
6 7 LANSING   3 DETROIT
8   4
ANN ARBOR   2 1
5

10

OHIO

TOLEDO 20   CLEVELAND   12
13   11
16   14   YOUNGSTOWN
15

18
19
COLUMBUS   7

21
DAYTON   MORGANTOWN
24

22 23
CINCINNATI   WEST VIRGINIA

HUNTINGTON
25

1   Detroit: Anna Scripps Witcomb Conservatory
2   Detroit: Moross House
3   Bloomfield Hills: Cranbrook
4   Ann Arbor: Matthaei Botanical Gardens
5   Tipton: Hidden Lake Gardens
6   East Lansing: The Gardens of Michigan State University
7   Lansing: Cooley Gardens
8   Midland: The Dow Gardens
9   Grand Rapids: Frederik Meijer Gardens

10   Niles: Fernwood
11   Cleveland: Cleveland Botanical Center
12   Kirtland: Holden Arboretum
13   Birmingham: Schoepfle Garden
14   Akron: Stan Hywet Hall
15   Mansfield: Kingwood Center
16   Canfield: Fellows Riverside Gardens
17   Newark: Dawes Arboretum
18   Columbus: Franklin Park Conservatory and Botanical Garden
19   Columbus: Park of Roses

20   Toledo: Toledo Botanical Garden
21   Dayton: Stillwater Gardens and Aullwood
22   Cincinnati: Cincinnati Zoo and Botanical Garden
23   Cincinnati: Krohn Conservatory
24   Morgantown: Core Arboretum
25   Huntington: Huntington Museum of Art, C. Fred Edward Conservatory

GREAT LAKES EAST:

Michigan, Ohio, West Virginia

We often think of the Midwest as an unvaryingly flat landscape covered with corn fields and dotted by small towns. To think of a place in sweeping, generalized terms is a common mistake. The eastern Great Lakes region, which is defined as the states of Michigan, Ohio, and West Virginia in this book, is not only expansive but encompasses an extreme diversity of landscape types, culture, and history.

Among the cities, Detroit has seen the greatest times and the worst times. The last twenty years have not been kind to the Motor City. A mass exodus to the suburbs has drained the downtown of human and financial resources. Large tracts of the urban core are abandoned. Wonderful, beautiful Victorian mansions lie in ruin, many half burnt to the ground. On the flip side, Detroit was once a great city, with a cultural life that rivaled Paris in the 1920s. The burnt-out buildings were once grand residences, and what remains is a provocative if somewhat painful reminder of the city's past grandeur. A small movement has been underway for some years to revive Detroit, and several of these old buildings have been renovated. Near the river, just a hop from the old Stroh's brewery (itself a majestic old industrial building that has been renovated) lies the Moross House, a lovely townhouse, surrounded by intimate urban-scaled gardens that epitomize the idea of a retreat from the harshness of the city.

Outside of Detroit lies one of the more significant gardens in the region, the Arts and Crafts landscape of Cranbrook in Bloomfield, Michigan. Originally carved from the

OPPOSITE: *Leila Arboretum entry way and fountain garden*

I

wilderness twenty miles north of downtown, Cranbrook's gardens are an attempt to meld human art with the grandeur of nature. The philosophy that pervades the school and is symbolized in the gardens does not grapple with these things as a duality in conflict, but as complimentary forces—man of nature, nature of man—to produce art that is seamless and simplified. Besides the landscape, this is expressed in the Institute's fine architecture and collections of sculpture and decorative arts.

The other major garden in this region is Stan Hywet in Akron, Ohio. Travelers will quickly perceive the kinship this early-twentieth-century mansion shares with other notable estates of the "country place era," a time when wealthy Midwestern industrialists built opulent country homes. Some were moving out from such urban centers as Cleveland, Chicago, and Detroit; some were raising their mansions in smaller towns on the middle plain. There may be no more historically important landscape in the Midwest than Stan Hywet, which, with its English accents and distinctly Beaux Arts American vocabulary, is considered a masterwork of landscape architecture.

Of course, many lesser known gardens merit attention. Nestled within the hills of West Virginia, on the campus of West Virginia University, is the Core Arboretum, which contains one of the best collections of naturalized Virginia bluebells around. The local botanical garden in Toledo sports an excellent shade garden, while the evolutionary plant display at the Michigan State University W. J. Beal Botanical Garden may be the most extensive, best produced such display in the country.

Although not plentiful, there are a few iconoclastic gardens in the region—landscapes that bear the unmistakable stamp of a loving personality. Two of these are worth mention. The Dow Garden in Midland, Michigan, resonates

with the spirit of Herbert Dow, founder of the chemical company that bears his name. From the striking architectural bridges to the quirky landscape "bumps" that roll silently across the grass, the garden brings us into the life of a single individual and shows how land can be one of the most intense vehicles for self-expression. The Schoepfle Garden in Birmingham, Ohio, is a quieter, less humorous place. Here we enter the world of Otto Schoepfle, consummate lover of plants, whose lifelong relationship with this small plot of land is great, subtle, and intimate. We are lucky he chose to share it.

The Great Lakes East, like all the regions of the Midwest, is too vast to tour entirely. Each place has its own character, whether it is derived from the soil, the topography, or the people. A characteristic that the gardens, in turn, visually embody.

OPPOSITE: *A Katsura (center) and magnolia (right) at the W.J. Botanical Garden at Michigan State University*

GARDEN OPEN: 10 am to 5 pm daily.

ADMISSION: $2 adults, $1 children under 13 years.

FURTHER INFORMATION FROM:
Belle Isle Park, Detroit 48207
(313) 852–4065

NEARBY SIGHTS OF INTEREST:
Belle Isle Zoo and Aquarium,
Doisin Great Lakes Museum

I Detroit: Anna Scripps Witcomb Conservatory

LOCATION: BELLE ISLE, AT LOTTER WAY AND INSELRUHE AVENUE, TWO MILES WEST OF DOWNTOWN

It was with a mix of excitement and trepidation that the city fathers of Detroit called on Frederick Law Olmsted to design a park on Belle Isle in 1881. They admired the landscape architect's work for Central Park and wanted a signature landscape too for this up-and-coming city. They also worried about the expense. Instructed to keep it inexpensive, Olmsted transformed the low-lying, swampy hump in the Detroit River into a dense urban forest, circumscribed by a simple path and canal system. In explaining his methods to the people of Detroit, Olmsted intoned they must keep a few "simple, distinct objects in view." One of these objects is a conservatory, designed by Detroit architect Albert Kahn almost twenty years later. Kahn's glasshouse was originally constructed in wood; in the 1950s the city undertook a major restoration and rebuilt it in steel. The conservatory renamed itself after the principal donor to this effort, Anna Scripps Witcomb, a member of the Michigan publishing family. The central dome rises 85 feet and houses large palms. Axial wings on the north and south contain tropicals and arids, respectively. The tropical collection focuses upon plants that have economic importance such as fruits and those used in industry. There is also an emphasis on displaying the lushness of tropical rain forests, to the effect that the South Wing can often seem jungle-like. The North Wing features a solid collection of cacti and succulents arranged methodically according to climatic associations. The main feature of the conservatory is the revolving cycle of seasonal flower shows. In the winter, there are cyclamen, cineraria, and kalanchoes contrasted with pink and white camellia trees. Spring showcases white lilies, early summer amaryllis, and fall mums; and Christmas culminates in an abundance of poinsettias. Part of the permanent display is given over to one of the largest collections of orchids in the country, featuring 5,000 plants, many donated by the Witcombs. Outside the conservatory are several small gardens

A summertime water garden, beside the conservatory, enlivens Olmsted's park.

that integrate with the park, although they defy Olmsted's instruction against flowering plantings in the landscape, which he felt would detract from the natural scenery. Among these are a lily pool garden, a rose garden, and a changing display of annuals and perennials set in free-flowing beds lined by grass.

2 Detroit: Moross House

LOCATION: EAST JEFFERSON STREET, ONE HALF MILE EAST OF
THE RENAISSANCE CENTER

GARDEN OPEN: 9:30 am to 3:30 pm Tuesday–Thursday; on Saturdays during special events. ADMISSION: free. Tours: $1.00.

FURTHER INFORMATION FROM: 1460 East Jefferson, Detroit 48207 (313) 259–6363

NEARBY SIGHTS OF INTEREST: Belle Isle, Detroit Institute of Art

The Moross House, built in 1843, represents urban Detroit's ancient history. The Greek Revival rowhouse was restored in 1969, and while the rest of the city has seen hard times a dedicated group of preservationists has overseen its survival. Behind the house, fitted into a tightly walled space, is a garden that was also restored in 1969. It was designed in the milieu of mid-nineteenth-century styles, with such heirloom plants as viburnums and climbing roses, set in a tightly controlled pattern of pathways and specimen trees, such as London planes and flowering crabapples. A patio, designed in 1974, uses bricks salvaged from old Beaubien Street when the Renaissance Center was built. A long pergola draped with ample wisteria sets the garden apart from the hubbub of the city streets, while the intimate scale and tall walls constantly remind one that this is indeed is an urban garden. In recent years the local garden society that administers the house and the gardens have been turning away from strict adherence to the restoration plan and have incorporated more contemporary plants. The goal has been to make the garden inviting to the general public, particularly to children who visit here in groups during the spring.

Among the coneflower and lobelia are carpets of mint, lavender, and lamb's ear—plants that appeal to adventurous children. Other amendments include a vocabulary of prairie plants, such as a witch hazel tree and a lilac. The central wedge of the garden that receives the most sun is also the locus of floral experiments, while the surrounding edges take a steady and serene approach. A flood of ajuga has overtaken the lawn that once gave a formal definition to the space, while the old kousa and lilac trees have been pruned into a flowing, naturalistic manner. On the street face, the front yard espaliered apple and pear trees. The garden curator relates that foreign visitors, particularly from England, respond most enthusiastically ("are enraptured," she says) to the small urban garden, which probably reflects the horticultural sensibilities of the English Cottage Garden movement early in the twentieth century. Within the urbanism of Detroit, the Moross House Garden provides a counterpoint and reminder of gentler things.

In the heart of Detroit, the Moross House garden provides an escape.

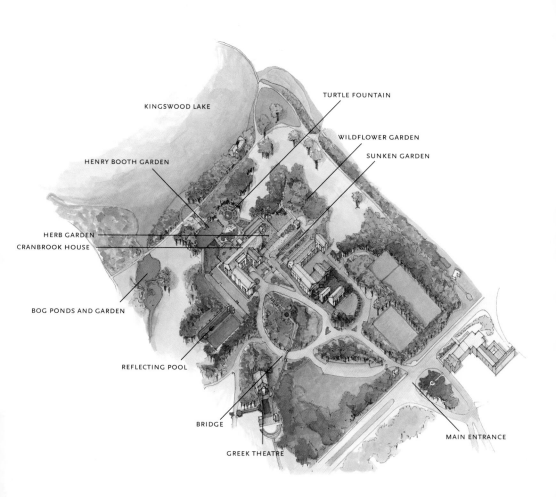

KINGSWOOD LAKE

TURTLE FOUNTAIN

WILDFLOWER GARDEN

HENRY BOOTH GARDEN

SUNKEN GARDEN

HERB GARDEN

CRANBROOK HOUSE

BOG PONDS AND GARDEN

REFLECTING POOL

BRIDGE

MAIN ENTRANCE

GREEK THEATRE

3 Bloomfield Hills: Cranbrook

LOCATION: LONE PINE ROAD, OFF WOODWARD AVENUE, SIXTEEN MILES
NORTH OF DOWNTOWN DETROIT

GARDEN OPEN: 10 am to 5 pm
Monday–Saturday, 11 am to 5
pm Sunday, May–August; 1
pm to 5 pm Monday–Saturday,
11 am to 5 pm Sunday,
September; noon to 4 pm
weekends, October. Closed
November– April. ADMISSION:
small fee is required.

FURTHER INFORMATION FROM:
380 Lone Pine Road,
Bloomfield Hills 48303-0801
(810) 645-3149
www.cranbrook.edu

NEARBY SIGHTS OF INTEREST:
Detroit Institute of Arts

George Booth belonged to that revolutionary breed of newspapermen at the turn of the century who, in conjunction with building empires, sought to better the world they lived in. Booth did not write his revolution, unlike contemporary William Cullen Bryant. Instead he crafted it, out of wood, metal, architecture, and landscape. Booth began life as a metalsmith and architect; in his early twenties he was conscripted into the newspaper business by his wife's family, the Scripps, owners of several Midwest newspapers. Under his tutelage the empire grew greater, and in short order Booth became a wealthy man. He turned his attentions in his leisure time to the arts and crafts of his youth, and set about building Cranbrook, an educational community that embodied in its principles and outlook the English arts and crafts movement, most notably its emphasis on the integration of art and science in daily life.

Several architects are associated with Cranbrook, most notably Albert Kahn and Eliel Saarinen. Yet Booth's aesthetic influence infiltrated everything, at times down to the detailing of furniture and fixtures. The 1907 house (attributed to Booth and Kahn) forms the spiritual centerpiece of the estate, with the educational community—now a private secondary school and several museums—spreading out in the valley around it. Many of the academy' structures are modernist masterpieces, including the copper-roofed girls school, while the main abode is a perfectly humble arts and crafts expression—with a rich collection of furniture and furnishings and surrounded by restrained but beautiful gardens.

To the east of the house are two intimate herb gardens, defined by brick walkways and low brick walls. These are intimate, residential spaces, meant to enclose the body and focus views inward. To this end there is a screen of cedars that forms a canopy and gives the area dimension. Stepping down, the garden opens into a formalized lawn terrace. A wall along the southern edge is capped with fruit-bowl bollards, then open views to a glorious sunken garden of bulbs arranged in vibrant geometric displays. Judging from the strict alignment of the diamond pattern, created in deep purple, pink, white, and yellow tulips, it is easy to make a connection between this garden and Saarinen's detailed architecture on the grounds, which features wondrously ornate patterning in everything from dormer windows to paving patterns. This garden is similarly mannerist, but reigns in any impulse toward eclecticism. In keeping with the arts and crafts emphasis on color and form joining in a cohesive manner, the central flower bed is bold . . . but not too bold. Surrounding the area, set against the dark rock retaining walls, is a loose

ABOVE: *A wealth of intricate arts and crafts details, such as this putti fountain, add majesty to Cranbrook's landscape.*

OPPOSITE: *A quiet dialogue between landscape and architecture underlies the design of Cranbrook.*

7

collection of peonies, lilacs, and other flowering shrubs that seems to enclose the garden and separate it from the house. This is a key tenet of garden design in the arts and crafts movement, particular to the work of William Robinson and Gertrude Jekyll, of which these gardens are somewhat derivative. Yet unlike the naturalistic gardens of the prairie style or of the ecological movement of the twenty-first century, the arts and crafts envisioned a middle ground between the organic state of the wild and the artificial works of man, a place where garden design could play with each of these extremes, toward its own coherent end.

A small terrace garden with a fountain at its center frames the north side of the house, wrapping around toward the west face. Close to the house lies the *Library Terrace* with a statue of "a gardener and his lady" surrounded by eight old bay trees meticulously pruned. Below this terrace is the most traditional garden—a long reflecting pool culminating in a grand display of peonies. The pool lies on an immense axis that runs up a hill toward the Saarinen-designed Academy of Art. Along its course westward, downslope from the house, lies an artful bog garden where students from the schools frequently congregate and relax. The use of native plant materials has always been a part of the landscape, and dates to a landscape plan designed by Ossian Cole (O. C.) Simonds between 1910 and 1923. Simonds laid out many of the roads that give the complex its ornamental farm character and designed the woodland areas as examples of prairie style landscape architecture. The *Bog Garden*, although not designed by Simonds, takes that philosophy and gives it an ecological updating. Stitched around three pools is a stand of maple and beech trees, underlain by a verdant carpet of hosta and lilies. Similar to this is a small wildflower garden located at the far end of the *Sunken Garden*, where trillium, ivy, and Japanese maples entwine around a stone fountain within the dark, moist confines of a

hemlock grove. The pinnacle of the naturalistic gardens at Cranbrook is reached within the *Oriental Garden,* which occupies a central position along the path between the house and the girl's school. An extension of the large lake in the middle of the campus creates the focal point for a selection of evergreens and hardy trees set in a prairie-like arrangement.

The rest of Cranbrook reads like a modernist garden of small architectonic courtyards, allées, and sculptural spaces. The most stunning of these are around the Academy of Art and the boy's school. Set upon cascading tier gardens, viewed through an arch in the building at the top, is a circular fountain adorned with the modernist sculptures of Carl deMille. Stepping through this space one gets a visceral sense of how landscape and architecture join to form a whole—an experience manifest throughout the entire campus. One of the best places to discover it is within the secluded *Greek Theater,* situated just south of the house, so that it is somewhat cut off from the rest of the campus. Here stands the best remnant of Simonds' single-species woodland, tightly wound around a small, open-air amphitheater, designed with perfect acoustics. Most people that visit this space do so alone, to quietly experience the art of it all.

ABOVE: *An Oriental bridge in midwestern character.*

OPPOSITE, TOP: *Garden ornament, drawn from classical and arts-and-crafts sources, frames a view of the prairie style landscape.*

MIDDLE: *A pebble-lined reflecting pool creates a serene setting.*

BOTTOM: *The Bog Garden is the newest addition to Cranbrook.*

4   Ann Arbor: Matthaei Botanical Gardens

LOCATION: DIXBORO AND PLYMOUTH ROADS, OFF U.S. 23, EAST OF DOWNTOWN

GARDEN OPEN: 8 am to sunset daily. ADMISSION: free. CONSERVATORY OPEN: 10:00 am to 4:30 pm daily, except major holidays. ADMISSION: $2 adults, $1 children 5–10 years, free children under 5 years; free 10:00 am to 1:00 pm Monday and Saturday.

FURTHER INFORMATION FROM:
University of Michigan
1800 North Dixboro Road
Ann Arbor 48105
(734) 998-7061
www.lsa.umich.edu/mbg

NEARBY SIGHTS OF INTEREST:
Cobblestone Farm, National Center for the Study of Frank Lloyd Wright

Although they are massive institutions, public universities live and die by their benefactors. Frederick and Mildred Matthaei endowed the University of Michigan with this magnificent garden. The Mattheai Botanical Garden, which serves as the school's research facility, is a maturing forest preserve on one hundred acres beside Fleming Creek. The garden is organized as a series of walks—several miles in all—through the native woodland. One walk, the Ethnobotanical Trail, features plants and vegetables used by native Americans in the Midwest and Southeast regions between 1000–1500 AD and includes a variety of indigenous corn, beans, and sunflowers. At the entrance to the arboretum stands a grove of bur oaks and red ash, an association that once covered this area of the Midwest before logging changed the landscape. Also in this area is a man-made wetland overflowing with wildlife—buzzing dragonflies to burping frogs.

A conservatory marks the entrance to the facility, containing a selection of tropicals, warm-temperate plants, and arid

Orchids, bromeliads, and other conservatory fare are part of the university's botanical collections.

plants set within a functional building. Ferns and succulents are special treats, with signage and members of the university's botany department at the ready to answer questions. Outside of the conservatory lie several formal garden areas, including a rose garden. Surrounded by a tall hedge, this mixture of perennial flowers and roses are presented both in the spirit of botanical and aesthetic education—labels and signs educate us, while the border garden design inspires us. There is also an eighteenth-century knot garden designed in an articulated style, with transverse axes, the central knot tightly woven in germander and santolina. Along the way into the arboretum is a small rock garden and a circular display of new world varieties, including a large collection of sunflowers inundated with butterflies in high summer. The gardens are a locus of research from disciplines far and wide; this past year a physicist was investigating how vegetation, specifically trees and grasses, mitigated the effects of radar for possible use around airports.

GARDEN OPEN: 8 am to dusk daily, April–October; 8 am to 4 pm daily, November–March.
ADMISSION: $1 weekdays year-round and winter weekends, $3 summer weekends.

FURTHER INFORMATION:
Michigan State University
Route M-50
6280 West Munger Road,
Tipton 49287
(517) 431-2060

NEARBY SIGHTS OF INTEREST:
Michigan Space Center,
Waterloo Farm Museum

5 Tipton: Hidden Lake Gardens

LOCATION: SEVEN MILES WEST OF TECUMSEH ON ROUTE 50

The Irish Hills were formed by the conjunction of two glaciers that met in this spot of lower Michigan about 10,000 years ago. In their retreat they left an unusual deposit of Canadian boulders and "funnel-like" depressions, which form the backdrop of the Hidden Lake Gardens. Comprising 755 acres of rolling land, the gardens were originally cultivated in the 1920s by local businessman Harry Fee, who began a nursery business on the site. When the national depression hit in the 1930s Fee reigned in his commercial activities; his primary interest was in the large-scale landscape and the way that planting trees and mowing fields affected one's perception of the topography. In 1945 Fee bequeathed the property to Michigan State University, and more traditional botanical activities began to take place. A pod-like conservatory, erected in 1968, contains tropical and arid collections. A small lath house features an exquisite selection of Japanese bonsai, the art of dwarfing conifers. Although there are ample oak-hickory woodlands, the outdoors is treated more as a succession of garden collections, a remnant of Fee's nurseryman's approach. Along the pathway system there is a smartly arranged dwarf conifer garden that is laid into a natural bowl of grass. According to the head gardener the point here is to educate everyday gardeners about the full range of small, yard-appropriate

The University of Michigan's gardens at Hidden Lake showcase native vegetation.

evergreens—"there's more to life than creeping juniper," he says, referring to the over 500 different specimens in the collection. The hosta garden is world-renowned, and is situated along a shaded stream. Farther along are crabapples, azaleas, lilacs, and cherries—all of which explode into bloom in their respective seasons. Drifts of perennials march across the lawn areas, giving focus to a landscape often seems much larger than it is.

6 East Lansing: The Gardens of Michigan State University

LOCATION: W. J. BEAL BOTANICAL GARDEN: NORTH CAMPUS, BETWEEN
THE MAIN LIBRARY AND IM SPORTS CIRCLE. HORTICULTURE DEMONSTRATION
GARDENS: SOUTH CAMPUS, CORNER OF WILSON ROAD AND
BOGUE STREET

GARDEN OPEN: Dawn to dusk daily. **ADMISSION:** free.

FURTHER INFORMATION FROM:
412 Olds Hall, East Lansing
48824-1047
(517) 355-9582

NEARBY SIGHTS OF INTEREST:
Kresge Art Museum, Fenner
Nature Center

Since the first plants went into the ground in 1873 the *W. J. Beal Botanical Garden* on the campus of Michigan State University has been about one thing: botany. Named after a director of the university's horticulture garden, the collections are laid out in a strict sequence of rectangular beds. First are the plant families, arranged in evolutionary sequence, starting with the evergreens and ending with dandelions—forty beds in

Michigan State's Horticultural Demonstration Garden provides design instruction and horticultural examples.

all. Winding around in one great swerve toward the Red Cedar River, the next fifty beds categorize their displays by their use, such as those employed in medicine or fibrous, aromatic, or edible plants. And for the darker sorts there is even an area dedicated to poisonous plants. Behind this main garden course is a mature arboretum of specimen trees that provide a verdant backdrop, shelter, and its own interest. Tucked into various corners of the long, meandering line of beds are specialty gardens, such as a display of endangered plants in the region. There are various species of grasses, such as Canadian burnet and rare goldenrod, as well as wildflowers, such as Jacob's ladder and tansies. As an educational institution, MSU's intent with this collection is for research and public education, in the hopes that a combination of the two might save the plants from extinction. There is also a bog area, working beds used by the horticulture department, and an area for shrub displays meant to enlighten and expand the mind of your average suburban gardener.

The *Horticultural Demonstration Gardens* take home gardener education to a new level. There are six areas, including a perennial garden, a rose garden, a test garden for new varieties and hybrids, an idea garden, a children's garden, and the foyer garden, which features plants appropriate for small spaces. The 4-H children's garden, designed by the foundation's director in conjunction with two university-trained landscape architects, is one of the more exiting educational gardens in the region, with displays planted to encourage children to learn about their natural environment. The entire garden is used by MSU as a pedagogical resource in its plant sciences and landscape architecture departments, and thus the displays are ever-changing.

7 Lansing: Cooley Gardens

LOCATION: SOUTH OF LANSING'S CENTRAL BUSINESS DISTRICT, CORNER OF MAIN AND TOWNSEND STREETS

This municipal garden was originally planted in the 1930s, upon a design by Michigan landscape architect Edward H. Laird. At that time this part of town was home to the local aristocracy, including industrialist Eugene Cooley, who donated the land. The garden was designed with a formal, Beaux-Arts-inspired structure of geometric hedges and shrubs, over which was laid an informal blanket of perennials. The flower design draws on the English cottage garden style, made popular in the early decades of the century by Gertrude Jekyll. Peonies proliferate, as do old style roses, irises, hydranges, and columbines. Within the intimate confines, there are also several classically arranged beds of annuals. In the 1960s, as rapid social changes affected Lansing, including the construction of an interstate that cut the town in two, this neighborhood entered a period of decline. Garden, naturally, reflected the changes and came near to demolition, but for the love and perseverance of a handful of citizens. The restoration, now over a decade in process, has reinvigorated this classic garden.

GARDEN OPEN: Dawn to dusk daily, year-round. **ADMISSION:** free

FURTHER INFORMATION FROM: P.O. Box 14164, Lansing 48907-4164 (517) 484-1880

NEARBY SIGHTS OF INTEREST: Woldumar Nature Center, Potter Park Zoo

Geometric hedges and shrubs frame this Beaux-Arts inspired garden.

8 Midland: The Dow Gardens

GARDEN OPEN: 10 am to sunset daily. ADMISSION: $3 adults, $1 children 6–17 years, free children under 6 years.

FURTHER INFORMATION FROM: 1018 West Main Street, Midland 48640 (800) 362-4874

NEARBY SIGHTS OF INTEREST: Midland Center for the Arts, Dow Museum, Chippewa Nature Center

LOCATION: CORNER OF EASTMAN AVENUE AND WEST ST. ANDREWS, DOWNTOWN MIDLAND, TWENTY MILES NORTHWEST OF SAGINAW

For some people landscape provides a soothing respite from the cares of the world. Just the sight of woodlands or a nicely cultivated garden calms the nerves. For others, landscape has the opposite effect, invigorating a creative spirit into action. This must have been the case with Herbert Dow, founder of Dow Chemical Company. On his estate in the hamlet of Midland, Dow let his imagination run wild with a fanciful landscape design. The centerpiece, at least in terms of whimsy, is an area of "bumps" where Dow and his gardener, Elzie Cole, carved the land into waving undulations. Elsewhere are several architectural follies, such as the vaguely chinoisserie red bridges that carry visitors over a small stream. More formal gardens are located close to the old Dow Homestead, which is now a national landmark. Besides the bumps, this area includes a rose garden, herb garden, and several displays of perennials. The emphasis is on experiencing the gardens; in self-guided walks, visitors are encouraged to leave the paths and tour the gardens close-up, crossing lawns and exploring the woods. The northern precinct of the landscape is given over to botanical research. Rhododendrons and azaleas are focal points, although there are several small beds of experimental flowers, an area of cultivated meadow, and an overlook in the flood plain of the Snake Creek that runs nearby.

The Dow Gardens reflect the character of their maker, Chemical founder Herbert Dow.

9 Grand Rapids: Frederik Meijer Gardens

GARDENS OPEN: 9 am to 5 pm Monday–Saturday, noon to 5 pm Sunday, year-round; 9 am to 9 pm Thursdays, summer months. ADMISSION: $5 adults, $4 seniors, $2 children 5–13 years, free children under 5 years.

FURTHER INFORMATION FROM: 3411 Bradford NE, Grand Rapids 49546 (616) 957–1580 www.meijergardens.org/home.html

LOCATION: EAST BELTLINE EXIT ON INTERSTATE 96, NORTH TO BRADFORD ROAD, EAST OF DOWNTOWN

Amalgams are not usually powerful. They lack purpose and direction. But sometimes a collection of disparate things comes together—typically under the auspices of a powerful personality. At this garden the personality is Fred Meijer, a wealthy Michiganite who was approached by a horticultural society to become a donor for a new botanical garden. Meijer saw it as an opportunity to showcase his growing collection of sculpture. The resulting gardens mix with intriguing effect large public botanical gardens with an outdoor art museum. The cornerstone of Meijer's collection is the representational work of Michigan artist Marshall Fredericks. Others in the outdoor collection include Dan Ostermiller and Alexander Liberman's

42-foot-tall abstract *Aria*. Many of the Fredericks' pieces are appropriately set within a new American garden of ornamental grasses and flowering perennials, designed by garden designers Wolfgang Oehme and James van Sweden, which highlights the Americana feel of his work. The arrangements work together so that the gardens play in harmony with the artwork. In a circle of English perennials and bulbs sits *Children Running Around the World*, an optimistic work by Midwest sculptor Kirk Newman. A conservatory on the grounds contains the largest collection of tropical plants in the Midwest. Orchids, bromeliads, and ferns comprise the first violins in this symphony. Henna and papyrus plants are curious additions, while the bottle palm (*Hyophorbe lagenicaulis*) takes the unusual prize, being native to a tiny island in the Mascarene Islands where only seven are living in the wild. Separated into its own room is a Victorian garden, where plants popular in the mid-nineteenth-century are grown. While botany was a popular pursuit among the European elite, a showy garden was also a provocative symbol of one's status, and this garden attempts to recreate the juxtaposition of exotic flora and handsome gardenesque design typical of small glass houses in this era. Fruits such as guava and oranges are featured, and in one corner rests a sculpture of herons by Gary Price.

The arid garden, with each desert of the world represented by geographic category, completes the collections. A campaign is underway to expand the gardens in the future. First on the list is the placement in late 1999 of *DaVinci's Horse*. The renaissance master was in the act of creating this monumental (24-foot-tall) equestrian statue when he died, and in conjunction with a group in Milan the Frederick Meijer Gardens has commissioned a casting according to the original drawing. It forms an important foundation upon which they hope to build a busy future.

Art and nature are the guiding themes of newborn Frederick Meijer Gardens.

10 Niles: Fernwood

GARDEN OPEN: 10:00 am to
6:00 pm Tuesday–Sunday,
May–September; closes at
7:30 pm in summer months;
10:00 am to 5:00 pm
Tuesday–Sunday, noon to
5:00 pm Sundays,
October–April. ADMISSION:
$4 adults, $3 seniors, $2 stu-
dents 13–19 years, $1 children
6–12 years.

FURTHER INFORMATION FROM:
13988 Range Line Road, Niles
49120
(616) 695-6491

NEARBY SIGHTS OF INTEREST:
Courthouse Museum, Warren
Dunes State Park

*A sensitive attention to
details, such as plant
layering, embody the spirit of
Fernwood.*

LOCATION: WALTON ROAD, EXIT 7 ON U.S. 31, ABOUT TEN MILES NORTH ON
INTERSTATE 80/INTERSTATE 90, ON THE INDIANA LINE

Fernwood began as the idealistic endeavor of a group of neighbors who wanted to purchase the land surrounding their
houses and maintain it as a nature preserve and garden. The
effort began in the 1960s, and today the 105-acre property,
known as Fernwood, remains a lovely oasis in the middle of
this rural area. The neighbors were impelled largely by the
financial resources of the Plim family and by the devotion and
knowledge of the Boyston family. Kay Boyston served for many
years as the garden's director and was responsible for planting
many of the gardens. Boyston's greatest impact is seen in the
wide diversity of plant and habitat, which has attracted a strong
wildlife population, notably 150 different bird species. Much of
the wildlife inhabits the nature preserve, which occupies a little
over one-third of Fernwood. The remainder is meadowed
arboretum or cultivated gardens. In keeping with the naturalistic theme of the property, the individual gardens are
approached as parts of a unified landscape, and thus flow into
and out of one another. In this way the garden is best seen as a
country estate, although in truth it was never a single, residential estate as such.

The entrance drive passes through the arboretum of a
mature canopy of trees set into a prairie meadow that is cut
back once a year. Mowed paths allow access, but the most common contact with the collections is by driving through. Beyond
the visitor center are the south gardens containing a terrace
garden and grand lawn with a vista over the preserve at the back
of the property. The terrace is formally designed with a geometrical boxwood pattern, a gazebo structure as a focal point at the
end, and annuals that attract butterflies and hummingbirds.
Educational displays include a *zero maintenance garden* of
seeded flowers that self-propagate as well as attract birds, which
serve to mitigate pest populations. There is also a *discovery garden* oriented to families, featuring exotic vegetables and a maze
for children.

Closer to the preserve, the landscape transitions into
shadier, informal areas. These include a *hosta glen, daffodil bowl,*
and *ravine garden* planted with a plethora of Japanese primrose
by Boyston 35 years ago. There are also thousands of wildflowers, sown years ago that have flourished into a lush tapestry of
color. The preserve contains miles of ecological trails with
markers describing the flora and fauna. Emerging, one passes
back through a rolling border landscape on the way back
toward the gardens. Here there is also a *hedge garden,* a *Japanese
garden* of raked gravel and landscape forms, and an *English cottage garden.* The Japanese garden is the closest Fernwood

comes to departing from the unified vision of Boyston and embracing garden rooms for the sake of garden rooms. But if one sees a connection between its hedge enclosure and that of the *hedge garden* farther downslope it makes sense, a part of the larger whole.

II Cleveland: Cleveland Botanical Center

LOCATION: UNIVERSITY CIRCLE, FIFTEEN MINUTES EAST OF DOWNTOWN PUBLIC SQUARE

GARDEN OPEN: dawn to dusk daily. ADMISSION: free.
LIBRARY OPEN: 9 am to 5 pm Tuesday–Friday, noon to 5 pm Saturday, 1 pm to 5 pm Sunday.

FURTHER INFORMATION FROM:
11030 East Boulevard, Cleveland 44106
(216) 721-1600

NEARBY SIGHTS OF INTEREST:
Cleveland Museum of Art, Auto-Aviation Museum, Western Reserve Historical Society

The Cleveland Botanical Center began as a collection of books and a humble boathouse located on Lake Euclid. Here, in 1930, a group of avid gardeners established one of the first public garden libraries in the country, impelled largely by Mrs. William G. Mather, whose Gwinn estate is considered a pinnacle of landscape architecture. The library became a locus of horticultural activity in Cleveland until 1959 when the little boathouse fell victim to a terrible flood. A new library was built in University Circle, near the art museum, and in 1966 the first in a "garland of gardens" was planted around the building. The *herb garden,* which the Western Reserve Herb Society donated and still maintains, is designed as an eighteenth-century knot garden. In the middle of the garden sits an iron sphere, around which are entwined large circles of common herbs, such as thyme and catamint. As it rests on axis with the great west window of the library's Clark Hall, this central planting area acts as a piece of sculpture or a painting that is best experienced from a distance. Up close, there are several beds of herbs that illustrate a variety of uses from industrial to culinary. Located in a ravine on-site is a *Japanese garden*. Descending down a series of steps, one is treated to the illusion of water cascading off a mountain, created by rocks and carefully arranged shrubbery. A stone pagoda acts as an architectural focal point, while a small circuit of paths providing the ambulatory experience central to a strolling garden such as this. There is also a *rose garden* and a small *wildflower garden* planted within a woodland copse at the Botanical Center. The best time to view the latter is in the early spring, when the first plants break through the last of the snow. The library contains a valuable archive of material on gardening. As has been its tradition, the center operates as an educational facility, hosting various events throughout the year, such as the well-known White Elephant Sale to raise money and promote horticultural values.

An Elizabethan knot garden lies just outside the windows of the library of the venerable Cleveland Botanical Garden.

GARDEN OPEN: 10:00 am to
4:45 pm Tuesday–Sunday.
ADMISSION: $4 adults, $3
seniors, $2 children 6–15
years.

FURTHER INFORMATION FROM:
9500 Sperry Road, Kirtland
44094-5172
(440) 946-4400
www.holdenarb.org

NEARBY SIGHTS OF INTEREST:
Indian Museum of Lake
County, Fairport Marine
Museum

12 Kirtland: Holden Arboretum

LOCATION: OFF HIGHWAY 6, TWENTY-FIVE MILES EAST OF CLEVELAND

Mining executive Albert Fairchild Holden loved nature and for a while considered bequeathing his fortune to the Arnold Arboretum in Massachusetts. Yet his sister prevailed on him to look closer to home, and in the 1930s, after his death, the Holden Arboretum commenced. The heart of the institution is the 3,100 acres of trees with over 5,400 varieties. The design is sensitive to aesthetics as well as the botanical interest in each plant and the ecological associations found in nature. For instance, one notable area includes a collection of pink and white mountain laurels, set within a grove of mature oak, beech, and maples. Also important are the hardy rhododendrons and the conifer and magnolia collections. The designed garden areas include a *Display Garden,* just a short walk from the visitor center, featuring a gathering of lilacs and viburnums. In spring months, a profusion of bulbs arrives on the scene, which inaugurates a continual rotation of bloom through the summer. Contained within this area is the *Hedge Garden,* which is organized as a botanical display featuring different sizes, shapes, and composition (watch out for thorns!) of hedges. A new *Butterfly Garden,* adjacent to the visitor center, includes ornamental grasses and perennials. On the other side of the center lies the crabapple garden, which blooms in May and August.

GARDEN OPEN: 8 am to dusk
daily. **ADMISSION:** free.

FURTHER INFORMATION:
12882 Diagonal Road,
La Grange 44050
(216) 965-7237

NEARBY SIGHTS OF INTEREST:
Oberlin College, Indian Ridge
Museum

13 Birmingham: Schoepfle Garden

LOCATION: MARKET STREET, JUST SOUTH OF ROUTE 113, FOUR MILES FROM LAGRANGE

All gardens are human expressions. Even large botanical gardens express cultural beliefs and values. Yet sometimes, small individual gardens that bear the unmistakable stamp of one person tend to be the most interesting—embodying ideas that are peculiar, iconoclastic, and even strangely normal. Otto Schoepfle was a devoted gardener who transformed his grandparents' small rural homestead into a natural preserve of undisturbed woodlands and plentiful gardens. Shoepfle so loved plants that he could fall head over heels for an unusual specimen. Several remarkable specimen trees dot the gardens, each accompanied by a story of how Shoepfle pursued some nurseryman or collector for years to secure it.

The gardens are laid out along a central grass path as distinct rooms. The path sets out from the bay window of the house, which Shoepfle added after purchasing the property in

1934. An old Ely crabapple tree in poor health marks the entrance, and was a favorite place of Shoepfle's to sit and observe his work in later years. The first garden, closest to the house, is the most colorful and vibrant—a *border garden* of mixed perennials, evenly organized along grass path. Shoepfle first planted this area prior to World War II and several of the species, such as the poppies, are offspring of original plants. The local parks department, which now maintains the gardens, flourishes much care and attention on this area, and it continues to dazzle since Shoepfle's death in 1992. *Holly Harem* is adjacent, a collection of American hollies and so named because there is one male plant (devoid of the telltale red seeds) for every fourteen females. Shoepfle planted the garden in the 1960s during a massive expansion; it is little changed, save the haphazard planting by birds dropping seeds nearby.

Farther along the central path are a number of topiaries, fashioned out of yew. Most of these Shoepfle purchased preformed and maintained himself. He also concentrated many of his favorite tree specimens in this area. The Metasequoia (dawn redwood) was planted in 1950 and one of the oldest of these trees in existence, the species having only been rediscovered in 1941. A venerable gingko tree is also nearby. At the end of the path lies a conifer garden, containing dwarf varieties and the highly expressive Japanese umbrella pine, which Shoepfle acquired from a local nursery after years of pressing. Intermingled with this gentleman's arboretum are several small flower collections, including a daylily trail and seasonal color beds containing cannas, begonias, and dahlias. In addition to the 20 acres of cultivated gardens, Shoepfle also owned 50 acres of woodlands along the Vermillion River, which is accessed by a maze of trails. At his death, Shoepfle left this garden as his lasting legacy. The park district has wonderfully preserved his spirit in the garden's maintenance and propagation. All the while a public place, you might feel as if you are entering one person's special world.

A subtle artistry resides in Otto Schoepfle's garden.

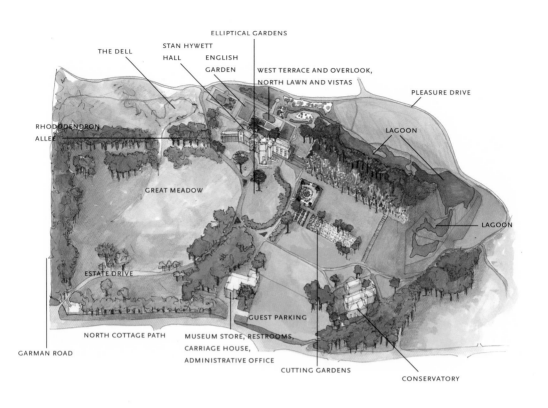

THE DELL

STAN HYWETT HALL

ENGLISH GARDEN

ELLIPTICAL GARDENS

WEST TERRACE AND OVERLOOK, NORTH LAWN AND VISTAS

PLEASURE DRIVE

RHODODENDRON ALLÉE

LAGOON

GREAT MEADOW

LAGOON

ESTATE DRIVE

GUEST PARKING

NORTH COTTAGE PATH

MUSEUM STORE, RESTROOMS, CARRIAGE HOUSE, ADMINISTRATIVE OFFICE

GARMAN ROAD

CUTTING GARDENS

CONSERVATORY

14 Akron: Stan Hywet Hall

LOCATION: PORTAGE PATH, OFF MERRIMAN ROAD, THIRTY MILES
SOUTH OF CLEVELAND

Stan Hywet (pronounced Stan HUGH-it) is a contradiction that just cannot escape itself. The Tudor style of the architecture was an attempt on the part of its patriarch, rubber tycoon Franklin A. Seiberling, at humility and a return to simpler values in his increasingly hectic modern world. And when considered alongside such other opulent country estates of its era, circa 1915, as the mansions of Newport or the grand creations of the du Ponts, one can see this is indeed true. But from today's vantage point, the red brick and sandstone manor house designed by Cleveland architect Charles S. Schneider contains nearly seventy rooms and was serviced by a small army of servants. Although the grounds are now just 71 acres, the original 3,000 acres could hardly have been considered self-effacing. The house features overt English overtones, reflecting an Anglophilia that extended into the landscape and gardens as well. For these, Seiberling hired Boston landscape architect Warren Manning. During the last decades of the nineteenth century, Manning worked in the office of Frederick Law Olmsted, where he was intimately involved with several major residential commissions, including the Biltmore estate in Asheville, North Carolina. The influence of Manning's work at Biltmore is clear at Stan Hywet.

Stan Hywet is laid out with careful attention to the vistas afforded by its location on a rise above the Cuyahoga River Valley that lies to the west. These are concentrated on the *West Terrace,* which lies just behind the house. Here, Manning created a descending savannah of formal lawns, capped by a graceful framing of trees that focus and concentrate the views. Like many historic estates, Stan Hywet suffered a period of neglect, during which the perimeter trees overgrew and destroyed the vista; restoration beginning in the late 1980s re-created views according to sketches and photographs maintained in the Manning archives. At the same time, Seiberling's grandson, U. S. Congressman John Frederick Seiberling (D-Ohio), secured much of the land in the lower valley for a protected refuge, thus preserving the views we enjoy today.

The focus on vistas of unfettered nature dominated English landscape architecture in the nineteenth century; however the single most English expression at Stan Hywet is the walled garden, known properly as the *English Garden.* Although English ideas of landscape were familiar to Manning, according to estate records he recommended the Seiberlings employ Ellen Biddle Shipman to design and construct this garden in 1929. The garden was originally intended as a sunny perennial garden. Over time nature determined

GARDEN OPEN: 9 am to 6 pm daily, except holidays. **ADMISSION:** $8 adults, $7 seniors, $4 children.

FURTHER INFORMATION FROM:
714 North Portage Path,
Akron 44303
(330) 836-5533
www.stanhywet.org

NEARBY SIGHTS OF INTEREST:
Akron Zoo, Goodyear World of Rubber

OPPOSITE: *Stan Hywet Hall,
1916*

BELOW: *Japanese architectural ornament focuses garden views.*

Mrs. Gertude Sieberling's favorite place was the English Garden, designed by Ellen Biddle Shipman in 1929.

otherwise, and as the trees surrounding this patch grew, shade subsumed the garden. In the 1980s an intrepid garden group undertook a restoration according to Shipman's original plans, making close approximations of her plant selections. The garden is focused inward on a fountain by sculptor Willard Paddock in 1916. Other architectural features include dry-set retaining walls, two roofed gates, and several garden pools. Perennials dominate the design, arranged in typical English cottage garden style, with its bold masses and impressionistic color contrasts.

Two of the most stunning allées in an American garden are located at Stan Hywet. One, the *Rhododendron Allée*, is unfortunately in poor shape, most of its stately London plane trees having died many years ago. A restoration using a disease-resistant variety of the same tree will take a long time before the original effect is recaptured. Nonetheless, the remaining rhododendrons (which at one point were layered with the plane trees) remain; and with a little imagination one can see how the allée was arranged to extend the axis of the house, which at this southern end, is culminated by the grand music room, a two-story architectural statement of grandeur. The other allée, a 550-foot double row of birch trees, continues this same axis on the north side of the house, connecting the manor to a congregation of picturesque teahouses. Birch is an unusual choice for this common feature of landscape architecture, as its irregular trunk seems antithetical to the purpose of creating straight lines. But this creates a fuller and more interesting construction, which, combined with haphazard stepping stones, makes this one of the most charming American gardens.

Below the vista from the West Terrace are two garden novelties original to the estate. The *Japanese Garden*, designed by the noted designer Otsuka, is typical of the era, during which a fascination for all things Asian consumed affluent patrons. Placed upon a cistern, the garden needs constant irrigation. Incongruously, the design incorporates plenty of water in a scheme that is intended to create a landscape in miniature scale. In this case the surrounding context is augmented, most notably with a facile rendering of Mt. Fuji in cast-concrete.

The name Stan Hywet means "stone quarry" in Old English, and refers to a pit found on the site during construction. Manning, sensing that this was an unusual feature that should be exploited, designed a *Lagoon Garden* in the area. Parts of the northern edge of the landscape were cleared in 1987 to open views across the valley, best grasped from the opposite side of the lagoon, where the vista is framed by the water feature and a carefully edited treescape. Adjoining the house is a small breakfast garden designed rather blandly (compared with the grandeur of the rest of the landscape) in a blue, white, and yellow color scheme reflective of the breakfast room that overlooks it. Following around to the southern end of the house is the dell, a nineteenth-century interpretation of an eighteenth-century picturesque woodland garden in the spirit of Andrew Jackson Downing. The pathway accentuates the dark, hidden nature of the landscape by literally bringing visitors below grade and through a romantic stone underpass that runs below the *Rhododendron Allée* and into the sunny meadow that fronts the property. The transition is at once simple and complex, qualities that describe the entire garden and connect it not only with the best traditions of landscape design but with the best in art in general.

TOP: *Warren Manning's bridges over the lagoon are icons of early-modern landscape design and the country-place era.*

BOTTOM: *The irregular birch tree formations make this allée one of the most magical American gardens.*

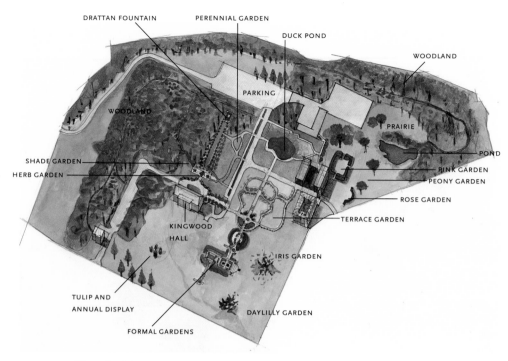

DRATTAN FOUNTAIN
PERENNIAL GARDEN
DUCK POND
WOODLAND
PARKING
WOODLAND
PRAIRIE
POND
SHADE GARDEN
HERB GARDEN
PINK GARDEN
PEONY GARDEN
ROSE GARDEN
KINGWOOD HALL
TERRACE GARDEN
IRIS GARDEN
TULIP AND ANNUAL DISPLAY
DAYLILLY GARDEN
FORMAL GARDENS

THIS PAGE: *Throughout the garden are vistas of the mansion.*

OPPOSITE: *Charles Kelley King's vaguely classical tastes have been combined into an eclectic garden.*

15 Mansfield: Kingwood Center

LOCATION: TRIMBLE ROAD, NEAR THE JUNCTION OF ROUTE 30 AND
INTERSTATE 71, SIXTY MILES SOUTH OF CLEVELAND

GARDEN OPEN: 8 am to 30 minutes before sunset daily, April–October; 8 am–5 pm daily, November–March.

HOUSE OPEN: 9 am to 5 pm Tuesday–Saturday, 1 pm to 5 pm Sunday, April–October; 9 am to 5 pm Tuesday–Saturday, November–March.

ADMISSION: free. Gardens and house closed on holidays.

FURTHER INFORMATION FROM: 900 Park Avenue West, Mansfield 44906. (419) 522-0211

NEARBY SIGHTS OF INTEREST: Fowler Woods

Charles Kelley King was a big man in a small town. As president of the Ohio Brass Company, King amassed a large fortune and settled in the sleepy little town of Mansfield in the 1930s, where he built his ample mansion. King was an avid gardener and surrounded his home with traditional gardens of various stripes. At his death in 1952 a trust was established to continue expanding and maintaining the gardens for the public. Since then the landscape has grown in fits and spurts, in several different directions, to the overall effect of creating a beautiful but somewhat disjointed aesthetic statement. A significant master plan has been developed in recent years that suggests several ways to stitch the diverse elements back together, and while some work has been undertaken in this direction, the gardens are still quite wildly different.

A tour begins in the woods where King designed several formal gardens, as if favoring seclusion and privacy rather than ostentation. These include an allée, a large terrace, and five independent rooms, differentiated by clipped hedges and dappled with contemporary sculptures, such as cherries on a cake. These spaces lie at the culmination of a series of terrace gardens that roll across the gently sloping landscape and are interpenetrated with stone fountains, blue stone terraces, and rings of exotic grasses and perennials, all set within a wide enclosure of native trees. This classically inspired area is the most European of the whole ensemble. Nearby sits King's French mansion, lying off axis and oriented toward a more informal grass allée that runs perpendicular to the terrace gardens.

Surrounding these formal areas are utilitarian gardens and greenhouses. In fact the major attraction over the years has not been the wonderful old fountains or blue stone terraces, but the large duck pond cut into the center of the gardens and overflowing with feathery friends. Much of this is how King wanted the garden to be. While old world opulence is noticeable in a few details, King's main emphasis at Kingwood was to create a place for the common man to commune with nature. As such there are many demonstration gardens that wrap around the property and culminate in the greenhouse complex at the eastern end, where a bustle of activity is always taking place. In the late spring, visitors from as far away as Cleveland travel down to see the working displays of croci, irises, and tulips that fill these structures and the gardens around them.

Today, the great threat to Kingwood is the commonness that King celebrated: suburban development completely surrounds the gardens, seeming each year to nip off an every dearer sense of seclusion. The new master plan makes efforts to reforest the woodlands around the property and re-design the entrance so that the visitor has less sense of the sprawl engulfing the area. Luckily a handsome woodland still protects Kingwood from development. Within this grove of Beech and Maple is a quiet trail that leads to a little visited, and hence sadly uncared for, shade garden of hostas and ferns. While as a garden it may lack a little verve, as a place away from it all, which is what drew Charles Kelley King here in the beginning, this is a little paradise.

OPPOSITE, ABOVE AND BELOW: *Demonstration gardens embody King's democratic sensibilities.* THIS PAGE: *Formal touches are hidden away from the center of the landscape.*

GARDEN OPEN: 10 am to dusk daily. **ADMISSION:** free.

EDUCATION CENTER OPEN: 10 am to 4 pm Monday–Friday, noon to 4 pm weekends, April–December. **ADMISSION:** free.

FURTHER INFORMATION:
7574 Columbiana-Canfield Road, Canfield 44406-0596
(330) 740-7116
www.neont.com/millcreek

NEARBY SIGHTS OF INTEREST:
Youngstown Museum of Industry and Labor, Lanterman Falls

16 Canfield: Fellows Riverside Gardens

LOCATION: PRICE ROAD, ON LAKE GLACIER, FIVE MILES SOUTHWEST OF YOUNGSTOWN

An infatuation with roses has overcome the good senses of many a gardener. Elizabeth Fellows was one of these. Yet unlike most rose gardeners Fellows had the sensibility to use the rose as an instrument in a larger concept. She did plant a formal garden of hybrid teas and floribundas, but you will also find roses scattered about as accents in perennial gardens as well. Fellows donated her property to the city of Canfield in 1958, and it has evolved into a major public garden. A major axis runs through the site and is designed as a mall, marked in the middle by a fountain surrounded by benches and fragrant annuals. On one side is an allée defined by a series of trellises covered with climbing roses and dahlias. A lush border of perennials runs along the length of the space, featuring hardy bulbs that are orchestrated into a cycle of bloom through the summer. On the other side of the fountain, the mall includes such blooming woody shrubs as crabapples. Formal *rose gardens* run along the allée. The collection is an all-America rose selection and is designed, plainly, in rows. A large axis through the center of the space connects with a lovely pavilion from where one can enjoy views of nearby Glacier Lake. Most of the garden areas, such as a Victorian gazebo planted in the middle of the garden, commemorate local gardeners, making this a gathering place of horticultural genius in northeastern Ohio. Beech trees dot the lawn that encompasses the center of the garden, leading the eye to the opposite end where contrasting views of industrial Youngstown can be had. There are also several specialty gardens here, including a *rock garden* of dwarf conifers that is spectacular in the winter and the *Blue Garden* of tipped hostas and blue-flowering annuals—a difficult garden to create, as those who have tried well know. Nestled into the woods across the mall is a new education center, which runs various classes and events in floriculture.

17 Newark: Dawes Arboretum

LOCATION: ROUTE 13, BETWEEN INTERSTATE 70 AND ROUTE 16, FIVE MILES
SOUTH OF NEWARK

GARDEN OPEN: Dawn to dusk
daily. ADMISSION: free.

FURTHER INFORMATION:
7770 Jacksontown Road SE,
Newark 43056-9380
(800) 44-DAWES
www.dawesarb.org

NEARBY SIGHTS OF INTEREST:
Octagon Earthworks, Black-
hand Gorge National Park

About halfway across Ohio, the terrain begins to roll somewhat between northeast and southwest, like a baritone clearing his throat before an aria—which in this case would be the mountains of Appalachia. Smack in the middle of this border country lies the sleepy interstate town of Newark. Beman Dawes came to Newark in 1896 to start a coal and coke business, succeeding to oil and natural gas, and then onto the U. S. House of Representatives. Dawes and his wife Bertie loved central Ohio and spent much of their time and energy cultivating a garden and arboretum on 1,100 acres of lake-pocked land. In 1929 Dawes opened the arboretum to the public, and since then it has grown into a wonderfully casual natural garden.

The most formal space is the *Japanese Garden*, designed by Makoto Nakamura in 1963. It is oriented around a central pond and includes such architectural features as bridges to focus views. The path system and pond have been re-engineered for the heavy visitor traffic. Elsewhere in the arboretum is an extensive, eight-acre *dwarf conifer garden,* in which plants are displayed in a variety of manners—some contrasted pleasingly against imported sandstone boulders, others strewn across large areas of lawn or resting in mulch beds. The underlying *parti* of the garden is an informal stroll through the woods. One emerges at periodic points into consciously designed areas, and then is immersed into the dense tree collections that dominate the site. The arboriculture has been organized by cultural (such as the Asiatic collection), nativity (many of the native Ohio specimens date back to Dawes), and taxonomy. The *Cypress Swamp* takes a prize for most unusual geographical landscape. Dawes planted it in 1928–1930 and now claims to be the northernmost bald-cypress swamp in the country. The undulating topography of this large swath of land creates some variation in climate from area to area, allowing a diversity of plants.

An ecologically sensitive boardwalk connects visitors with the Dawes Arboretum.

18 Columbus: Franklin Park Conservatory and Botanical Garden

GARDEN OPEN: 10 am to 5 pm Tuesday–Sunday, 10 am to 8 pm Wednesday. **ADMISSION:** $5.00 adults, $3.50 seniors and students, $2.00 children 2–12 years.

FURTHER INFORMATION FROM: 1777 East Broad Street, Columbus 43203-2040 (614) 645-8733 www.fpconservatory.com

NEARBY SIGHTS OF INTEREST: Wexner Center, German Village

LOCATION: CORNER OF EAST BROAD STREET AND NELSON ROAD, IN FRANKLIN PARK, ON THE EAST SIDE OF COLUMBUS

Constructed in 1895, the Franklin Park Conservatory is one of the oldest glasshouses in the Midwest. Its Victorian roots are evident in the architecture: ornate steepled dome, transverse wings, and a mile of delicately paned glass. But in spirit this is an American institution, and home to one of the bigger horticultural expositions in the country, Ameriflora, to which designers nationwide flock annually. The permanent collections are botanical and artful. The *Palm House,* the oldest part of the building, rises 55 feet from the ground and houses an ample collection of venerable palms. There are several outdoor garden areas located within courtyards between the wings. These include a patio of succulents, a bamboo grove, magnolias, and a small courtyard of bonsais. The two wings of the conservatory feature different ecosystem displays arranged as walking tours. In the north wing there are desert, tropical rain forest, and Asiatic mountain ecosystems, while the south contains a Pacific Island water garden and South American mountain forest. Extending in a linear five acres from the doorstep of the conservatory is the showpiece of the outdoor gardens, a wide strolling promenade lined with bright annuals, that is known by the clunky name of the *mallway.* At the center of the walk is the monumental Stephen Canneto sculpture *Navstar92.* The large sail of the work points toward the north star, and its 40-degree inclination signifies the city's relationship to the heavens (it lies on latitude 40 north). Outdoor gardens ring the conservatory, including a five-acre Japanese garden and several demonstration gardens. The *Victory Garden* will transport older visitors back to the era of World War II when citizen were encouraged to cultivate their own gardens to reduce consumption of goods and vegetables needed overseas and also as gesture of patriotism. Expect to see cabbages and other vegetables lightened by roses and other airy flowers.

The Grand Mallway focuses upon Navstar92.

19 Columbus: Park of Roses

LOCATION: CORNER OF HIGH STREET AND HOLLENBACK DRIVE, IN WHETSTONE
PARK, DOWNTOWN

In 1954 the American Rose Society packed their bags and relocated from Hershey, Pennsylvania, where they had been
ensconced at the Hershey Gardens, to Columbus. They took up
residence at the newly planted municipal rose garden here.
Although the Society has since moved to Shreveport, Louisiana,
the garden remains. The main gardens are laid out in a geometric matrix of formal rooms. Everything is here, from outrageous experiments in hybrid teas that push the envelope of
color and size, to the creepers and old varieties that blow your
mind with their perfume. In all, there are 13 acres of 11,000
bushes and 375 varieties. The heritage (old) roses are segre-
gated to their own area, as they are considered part of the whole
rose competition. In recent years an herb garden and bulb have
been added to the garden's mission, although roses remain—
and well they ought—the central purpose. According to a local
historian, creating this garden was no small feat for the city in
1951, requiring 21,000 bales of peat moss just to prepare the
ground. But the city fathers saw the garden as a way to create a
new public gathering space that could also function as a signature landscape. It remains that today, as people flock to the gardens every day, especially at the height of rose season, in mid
June and again in mid September.

GARDEN OPEN: Dawn to dusk
daily. ADMISSION: free.

FURTHER INFORMATION FROM:
440 West Whittier Street,
Columbus 43215
(614) 645-3300

NEARBY SIGHTS OF INTEREST:
Wexner Center, Center of
Science and Industry

*Columbus civic pride has
guided the development
of the Park of Roses for over
forty years.*

20 Toledo: Toledo Botanical Garden

GARDENS OPEN: 8 am to 9 pm daily, April–September; 8 am to 5 pm daily, October–March.
ADMISSION: free.

FURTHER INFORMATION FROM:
5403 Elmer Drive,
Toledo 43615
(419) 936-2986

NEARBY SIGHTS OF INTEREST:
Wolcott House Museum,
Art Museum

LOCATION: ELMER DRIVE, EAST OF EXIT 13 ON INTERSTATE 475, ON THE WEST SIDE OF TOLEDO

In the 1980s a severe economic slump hit Toledo, forcing many public parks to close. The Toledo Botanical Garden survived, through a public/private partnership. The garden, which began with the donation of 20 acres of land by a local businessman, has subsequently attracted most of the nonprofit arts and educational institutions to this little corner of Toledo. One area of the garden is given over to a village of buildings, where a local artists' club, several studios and galleries, and even a stained-glass guild make their home. The rest of the property contains gardens, spread across a landscape of lawns, groves, and public sculpture. Tours, either self-guided or by a docent, begin in the shade garden where varieties of hosta, ferns, and wildflowers are planted under the protective canopy of mature oaks. A small opening of sunlight graces an aquatic garden of water lilies set into a manmade pond. At the entrance of this garden sits the clay sculpture *Phoenix Cairn* by Laurie Spencer encircled by crocii.

The herb garden, farther along the path, is maintained by a local herb society and features, besides horticultural displays, an Elizabethan knot garden, a selection of Shakespearean herbs, and Bible garden. The main anchor to the botanical garden is the new perennial garden, designed by the Pittsburgh firm Environmental Planning and Design. A wall of arborvitae and yew surrounds this series of small rooms. A main border garden slices through the center. On the eastern side are arranged the color gardens—blue, white, pink, and red—the lilies, and the peonies. To the west is a typical cottage garden, which contains an assortment of perennials designed in broad strokes in the vein of the English style defined by Gertrude Jekyll. A new addition to the garden, the *Grand Allée*, lies adjacent to the perennials and is designed in double rows of silver leaf lindens, culminating in a semi-circle of crabapples. Educational displays pepper the parklike landscape that revolves around Crosby Lake, named after the gentleman who originally donated the land. Because of its prominence as the city's oldest and perhaps best maintained park, the botanical gardens are well-used on summer weekends.

Beauty in the landscape has attracted many local cultural institutions to the Toledo Botanical Garden.

21 Dayton: Stillwater Gardens and Aullwood

LOCATION: SIEBENTHALER DRIVE, BETWEEN NORTH MAIN STREET AND NORTH DIXIE DRIVE, EXIT 57B ON INTERSTATE 75

GARDENS OPEN: 8 am to dusk daily. ADMISSION: free. CENTER OPEN: 9 am to 5 pm Monday–Friday.

FURTHER INFORMATION FROM: 1301 East Siebenthaler Avenue, Dayton 45414-5397 (513) 277-6545

NEARBY SIGHTS OF INTEREST: Riverbend Art Center, Dayton Museum of Natural History

The city of Dayton began planting and building these gardens in the 1960s when local philanthropist Benjamin Wegerzyn donated 1,000 shares of Xerox in order to fund a horticultural center. For twenty years the little greenhouse facility and botanical library functioned solely on the generosity and pluck of the local "garden ladies," but in the early nineties the regional parks department, which administers acres of exquisite park land in and around the city, took over. Since then, the Wegerzyn Horticultural Center has been lovingly transformed, most notable by the addition of an outdoor garden area named for the Stillwater River that runs nearby. The central space of the garden is a handsome bowling green, bookended by the *North* and *South Plazas* at either end. The green is meant to strolled around, and is thus flanked by border gardens of perennials, defined and edged by lines of yew hedge. The plazas are circular flower gardens that offer excellent vistas of the green and surrounding landscape. The North features grasses and rugosa roses in a layered display, while the South finds daylilies mingling with black-eyed Susans and other perennials flowers and grasses. Along the eastern edge of this linear garden space are arranged several small garden rooms that display several formal gardening traditions. The first is the *Federal Garden*, with French-inspired brick terraces and boxwood parterres. At each end are two arches covered over with trained European beech trees. The *English Garden* is a fragrant paradise, with drifts of thyme, lavender, and perennial flowers combined in a freeflowing manner. The centerpiece of the space is a wooded pergola, from which one can view the flashy colorful designs of bedded-out annuals in the *Victorian Garden*. During normal springs the eastern edge of the gardens becomes a wetland garden. A new boardwalk that winds between the blackberry bushes and maple-ash forest has just been completed. The Wegerzyn Horticultural Center is an active force in the Dayton community and fills its summer evenings with workshops and educational programming.

A federal style garden elides with English traditions as part of the educational garden design at Stillwater Gardens.

With the metropark system there are several public woodlands and parks, including the richly designed naturalistic garden called *Aullwood*. The name is derived from John and Marie Aull, who first purchased this rolling 150 acres along

the Stillwater River in 1909. Unlike their neighbors, the Aulls were not farmers, in fact they regretted the effects of agriculture on the native landscape and spent much of their time and resources converting their land into the native woodlands and meadows of wildflowers. In the spring, catch the thousand of Virginia bluebells that fill the woods with a vibrant blue carpet. A major feature of the garden is the stream that cuts through the property, carving several ravines along its length and serving as a touchstone for any stroll through the woods. Many of the stone dams and retaining walls date back to the thirties and forties and were constructed by John Aull himself. While in all seasons the eye alights up some raucous population of flowers, the main attraction to the garden for Marie Aull was always the handsome woodlands—a diverse array of ash, oaks, maples, and native hawthorns.

GARDEN OPEN: 9 am to 8 pm daily, summer months; 9 am to 7 pm daily, fall, winter, and spring. **ADMISSION:** $10.00 adults, $7.00 seniors, $4.75 children 2–12 years.

FURTHER INFORMATION FROM: 3400 Vine Street, Cincinnati 45220 (513) 559-7734

NEARBY SIGHTS OF INTEREST: Cincinnati Art Museum, Taft National Historic Site

22 Cincinnati: Cincinnati Zoo and Botanical Garden

LOCATION: DRURY AVENUE, ON THE NORTHERN EDGE OF THE CITY, ACCESSIBLE BY METRO BUS

Today the newest thing in zoos is "immersion experience." Gone are the wire cages and cement boxes that once housed unhappy and sick gorillas, rhinoceros, and other exotic wildlife. Instead, the habitats are being designed to approximate the animals' native ecosystem. At the same time, zoo design—using safety glass and high tensile wire—aims to bring the visitor into much closer contact with this world. We walk underneath, dangle over top of, and at times feel perilously close to the animals. Naturally a big component of this revolution is landscape design. In some ways zoos are becoming more like naturalistic botanical gardens. The Cincinnati Zoo has been this way for a long time, and in fact considers itself as much a garden as a zoo. Unlike botanical gardens that arrange plants according to scientific type, all the displays here are based upon ecosystem associations. In the gorilla habitat expect to see big leaf magnolia, bamboo, and Akebia—all components of the animals' diet. A new manatee exhibit is designed like a Florida mangrove wetland, and host alligators and turtles, as well as the lumbering main attraction. In addition to these animal exhibits, there are several decidedly gardenesque areas at the zoo, including The *Garden of Peace* that contains plant species from the Fertile Crescent and Israel. A small wetland of papyrus and rushes sits pleasantly ensconced beneath a grove of Lebanese cedars and Cilician firs.

In some ways the zoo has always regarded landscape as a primary mission, dating back to its creation 125 years ago

when it was planted as an experimental garden. A few remnants of this history still remain on-site, including the Japanese pagoda tree (*Sahpora japonica*) sitting near the entrance, the 200-year-old red oak and pin oak at the gazebo, and the oversized catalpa between Swan Lake and the education center. Currently this focus upon exotic landscape has been updated by the construction of the *Gertrude MacRae McIlwain Endangered Species Garden*. The garden is organized into four sections—prairie, woodland, wetland, and rocky freshwater shorelines, which have been dramatically lost over the century—particularly on the lakes in the Midwest—through extensive quarrying. The wetland is specifically a sphagnum bog, also a narrow category that has succumbed to rapidly sprawling suburbs. Two arboretum-like gardens are located within the zoo. The *Oriental Garden* is actually more of a pinetum, feature mostly Asiatic conifers, designed as a small forest. The Jungle Trail contains many rare plants from the tropical rainforests over the world, animated in this case with a motley assortment of monkeys and apes.

Gardenesque habitats have made the Cincinnati Zoo as much a place of flora as fauna.

The zoo has received many awards over the years, including several for its gardens. One of these, the Green Survival Award, signaled out the landscape collections for their dedication to conserving plant diversity.

23 Cincinnati: Krohn Conservatory

LOCATION: EDEN PARK, DOWNTOWN

At the turn of the century Cincinnati wanted to build a major conservatory to rival its midwestern competitors—notably Chicago and Pittsburgh. But unlike those cities, Cincinnati lacked a single wealthy donor to make it happen. A small greenhouse was located in Eden Park in 1902, but it was not until 1930 that a full-fledged conservatory was erected. Architects Rapp and Meachem designed the Krohn Conservatory, named after a superintendent of parks. In 1966, after a storm damaged much of the building, a major restoration was undertaken, lead by the New York glasshouse firm Lord and Burnham, venerable designers and builders of many turn-of-the-century conservatories along the east coast. Here, they replaced all the wood with aluminum, and fitted the structure with over 14 tons of new glass. Amazingly, during construction no plants were relocated, and instead the entire process took place around the collections, which continued to grow through

GARDEN OPEN: 10 am to 5 pm daily, 10 am to 6 pm Wednesday. ADMISSION: free.

FURTHER INFORMATION FROM: 950 Eden Park Drive, Cincinnati 45202 (513) 352-4080

NEARBY SIGHTS OF INTEREST: Cincinnati Museum of Art, William Taft National Historic Site

the summer—so well, in fact, that many had to be cut back.

There are five permanent gardens that comprise the conservatory. These include the *Palm House*, located beyond the lobby in a kind of sunken living room. This collection was begun with the purchase in 1902 of some 380 varieties made in Philadelphia, which soon became the largest collection of palms west of there. Several existing plants are descended from that first garden. The *Tropical House* features cycads and other rainforest varieties arranged taxonomically. There is also a *Desert House* and two gardens of bonsai. The main feature at the conservatory is found in the show room, where major horticulturists and garden designers perform seasonally. A general schedule is adhered to (bulbs and flowering trees in the spring, annuals in the summer, mums in the fall, poinsettias at Christmas); however the designers are given latitude for full expression. A special emphasis is made to display a Midwest sensibility, and there are several shows each year that inevitably push the envelope of a nascent renaissance in heartland gardening.

A waterfall forms the centerpiece of the Krohn Conservatory.

GARDEN OPEN: Dawn to dusk daily. **ADMISSION:** free.

FURTHER INFORMATION FROM:
P.O. Box 6057, Morgantown 26506-6057
(304) 293-5201

NEARBY SIGHTS OF INTEREST:
Cooper's Rock

24 Morgantown: Core Arboretum

LOCATION: EVANSDALE CAMPUS OF WEST VIRGINIA UNIVERSITY, ROUTE 19, THREE MILES EAST OF MORGANTOWN

The Core Arboretum, like many academic institutions, started out to propagate exotics from around the world in a controlled, garden-like setting as an intellectual exercise. The point was to amass a significant worldwide collection as well as to study science. Compared with other arboreta the Core was only moderately successful in this mission, due in large measure because nature interceded. The site is located at the edge of the West Virginia University campus where the land slopes off precipitously toward the Monongahela River. The rich soil of this hillside has become the setting for a magnificent showcase of spring-blooming wildflowers that, in the words of a resident botanist, "will knock your socks off." The star of the show are the thousands of Virginia bluebells (*Mertensia pulmonarioides*) that burst on the scene in mid-April. Other varieties vie for attention throughout the season, which begins in certain years

in late March and can extend as late as the end of May. The rest of the arboretum contains mainly native woody and herbaceous plants that are managed but not planted. Several miles of foot-paths await the energetic visitor, while volunteers from the biology department are usually on-hand during the week to give tours and answers questions.

A carpet of bluebells subdues the West Virginian woods at the Core Arboretum

25 Huntington: Huntington Museum of Art, C. Fred Edward Conservatory

LOCATION: EXIT **8** OFF INTERSTATE **64**, NORTH ON **152** TO MILLER ROAD

GARDEN OPEN: 10 am to 5 pm Tuesday–Saturday, noon to 5 pm Sunday. ADMISSION: free.

FURTHER INFORMATION FROM: 2033 McCoy Road, Huntington 25701 (304) 529-2701

NEARBY SIGHTS OF INTEREST: Antique Radio Museum, Railroad Museum

Enclosed within this art museum is a gem of a conservatory. While most museum gardens present a formal image (like a piece of art), this conservatory is designed to be experienced. An informal pathway winds through the 3,100-square-foot space. The permanent collection features subtropical species arranged according to the taste of the curator, Liz Dolinar, not taxonomically. It includes mostly flowering shrubs, such as fox-tail palms, tree ferns, and orchid trees. In the center of the space resides *Play Days,* a bronze sculpture by Harriet Frishmuth. In one area there is room for seasonal displays, which the curator designs with horticultural aplomb. Expect to see poinsettias at Christmas, mums in the fall.

Small, inclusive spaces connect in an experiential garden at the Huntington Art Museum.

1 Chicago: Gardens of the Art Institute	10 Rockford: Klehm Arboretum	17 Indianapolis: Garfield Park Conservatory and Sunken Gardens
2 Chicago: Lincoln Park Conservatory and Gardens	11 Rockford: Anderson Gardens	18 Indianapolis: Indianapolis Museum of Art
3 Chicago: Garfield Conservatory	12 Rock Island: Quad City Botanical Center	19 Fort Wayne: Headwaters Park
4 Oak Park: Oak Park Conservatory	13 Moline: Butterworth Center and Deere-Wiman House	20 Fort Wayne: Foellinger-Freimann Botanical Conservatory
5 Evanston: Shakespeare Garden	14 Peoria: George L. Luthy Memorial Botanical Garden	21 Columbus: Irwin Home and Gardens
6 Willmette: Bahai Temple	15 Springfield: Lincoln Memorial Garden	22 Muncie: Oakhurst Gardens
7 Glencoe: Chicago Botanic Garden	16 Springfield: Washington Park Botanical Garden	
8 Lisle: Morton Arboretum		
9 Wheaton: Cantigny		

GREAT LAKES WEST REGION:

Illinois, Indiana

As many gardeners might suppose, Chicago dominates the garden scene in this part of the Midwest. It is a major city with the public and private infrastructure to support a number of important gardens. The Chicago Botanic Garden, located on the lake shore north of the city, is the most prominent. With 385 acres of formal and landscape gardens, it is the largest garden in the area; yet at just thirty years old it is also one of the newest. Within the city of Chicago and its immediate suburbs are three important historic conservatories. Jens Jensen, a Danish-born landscape architect whose "prairie style" revolutionized gardening in Chicago, designed Garfield Conservatory on the west side in the 1910s. Filled with lush tapestry of tropical plants, the conservatory amazed residents of this cold, northern metropolis with its exotic array. Thanks to its success, the Lincoln Park and Oak Park Conservatories followed shortly thereafter. Each building is relatively small when compared with contemporary domes and glasshouses, and objectively the architecture of each is quite uninspired. Yet these are some of the most intimate and forgotten spaces in the city, each of which has been artfully designed by either a skilled landscape architect (Jensen) or a knowledgeable gardener imitating his influential lead.

As the population and geography of Chicago grew exponentially in the first decades of this century, great estates arose on its outskirts. Today, two of these are home to wonderful gardens. One, the Morton Arboretum, is a large academic institution containing a world-renowned collection of trees on what was once the

OPPOSITE: *A gentle opening creates a subtle space at Cantigny in Wheaton, Illinois.*

private residence of salt magnate, Joy Morton. Cantigny, located only a few miles away, features wonderfully maintained formal flower gardens, a stately landscape, and the museum home of Robert McCormick, monarch of the *Tribune* publishing empire.

Chicago's founders adopted the motto *Urbs in Horto—City in a Garden—* when they incorporated this town of the middle west in 1837. Over the years, various mayors, including most recently Richard M. Daly, have devoted much expense to keeping the city well stocked in flowering median strips and attractive parks. The centerpiece of all this activity is Grant Park, with a number of different flowerbeds, including some showy bedded-out annuals at specific entrances. On the edge of the park is the Art Institute of Chicago, flanked on each side by courtyard gardens. Although not typically thought of as gardens, these spaces are so intelligently designed and make such strong aesthetic statements that they are featured on page 43 as one of the finest garden experiences in the city.

The influence of Chicago can be felt far into the countryside, particularly in Jen Jensen's impact on midwestern gardening sensibilities. One of the highlights of a visit to Springfield, Illinois, is the Lincoln Memorial Garden, designed by Jensen in the 1930s.

Indiana is made of much more than Hoosier-frenzied university boosters, agribusiness, and Republican politics. The state boasts impressive gardens and public landscapes. Of the latter, two important parks are included in the following pages precisely because they represent a certain "gardenesque" view of how a public park should function. Just as Frederick Law Olmsted observed 150 years ago when selling his concept for Central Park in the heart of New York City, people living in towns and urban situations need a direct connection with

nature. Although aesthetically different, Garfield Park
in Indianapolis and Headwaters Park in Fort Wayne
present a unique vision of how natural landscape can
be integrated into the urban context.

Several industrialists have left a lasting legacy
in Indiana, and their vast estates have survived in varied form down to the present day. The Landon family
residence in Indianapolis now houses the local art
museum, and the Italianate gardens have been augmented with modern sculpture to create an intriguing
and continually beautiful pastiche of history. The Ball
compound in Muncie thrives as a cultural center, and

*At Foellinger-Freimann
Botanical Conservatory in
Fort Wayne, volunteers
engage chidren in gardening
pursuits.*

the intimate, personal gardens of
Elizabeth Ball are now being
expanded with an eye towards public
education and ecological restoration.
In Columbus, Indiana, the Irwin
family continues to occupy their
Italian gardens, designed in 1910 by
the architect Henry Phillips.
Although still in private hands, the
Irwins graciously open their special
landscape to the public.

A tradition of public botanical gardens continues to thrive in

this region. New botanical gardens have opened in recent years in Rock Island, Illinois, and Fort Wayne, Indiana, while older civic glasshouses are being restored elsewhere—most notably in Garfield Park in Indianapolis.

When people speak of America's *heartland* they inevitably have an image in mind of cornfields, little league baseball, and quiet sunsets. It is an image most properly of Indiana and Illinois. Here the landscape of rolling farms finally casts off its eastern pretensions and settles into the easy, flat rhythm of the Midwest. Although some vestiges of traditional European garden-making can be found here and there, gardens in these two states express a homegrown sensibility, whether aesthetically, such as in the prairie style of Jensen, or philosophically, such as in the idea that every decent town ought to have a botanical garden.

Chicago: Gardens of the Art Institute

LOCATION: ART INSTITUTE OF CHICAGO, MICHIGAN AVENUE AT ADAMS STREET, DOWNTOWN

GARDEN OPEN: dawn to dusk daily. ADMISSION: free.

FURTHER INFORMATION FROM:
111 South Michigan Avenue,
Chicago 60603
(312) 443-3600
www.artic.edu

NEARBY SIGHTS OF INTEREST:
Grant Park, Sears Tower, Navy
Pier, the Museum Campus

The Art Institute of Chicago is one of the most important art museums in the country, housed in a building that meets that challenge. Designed by Shepley, Rutan, and Coolidge for the Chicago World's Fair in 1893, this Beaux-Arts structure rises along Michigan Avenue (on the Grant Park side of the boulevard—the only building to do so) as a testament to the city's gilded *fin de sciele* history. Inside, the building seems enormous; from the street outside, however, it appears smaller than similar institutions (the Field Museum nearby, the Cleveland Museum of Art, or New York City's Metropolitan Museum, for instance). This is because of a sensitive siting of the building close to Michigan Avenue and the design of a handsome entrance stairway. Flanking the entrance to the north and south are beautiful mature gardens that are also designed to the urban scale.

The gardens to the south were created by the modernist landscape architect Dan Kiley. The garden—or *courtyard* perhaps is a better term—vaguely replicates the ordered *parterres* of French Renaissance gardens with an arrangement of granite planters, a fountain and rectangular pool, and the mercantile sculpture of Loredo Taft, which depicts the humanizing of the Great Lakes in an American neoclassical vocabulary. While the architecture is massive and strong, after more than two decades the most impressive features of the space are its square shape and intimate scaling, achieved primarily by the dense covering of hawthorns Kiley planted in a studded grid; these have thatched together to create a prickly covering just six feet above

The South Garden of the Art Institute is composed as an intimate, modernist grove of low-lying hawthorns.

the ground. They shade the gardens, making the colors resonate, a subtle mixture of silver granite and orange gravel, deep green vinca twining up the trunks of the native hawthorns, and the faintest red glow of impatiens placed in the planters during summer. The garden has an ineffable presence: something musky, something conscious but quiet.

To the north of the stairs lies a more architectonic modern garden designed by landscape architect Laurie Olin in the 1980s. The museum obviously intended this garden to house modern sculptures from the last half of the century, and therefore, structurally, it is strongly differentiated from the southern garden. However, by employing the same material vocabulary of that space—orange gravel, vinca, and canopy trees—Olin makes a serious reference to Kiley, even if his design marks a radical departure. A central panel of grass defines the garden, upon which a bright orange Alexander Calder sculpture rests at one end, while a burnished steel construction by David Smith sits at the other. This is an art museum garden, after all. A smaller panel of vinca is overlaid on the turf panel, encompassing the Calder. Against this lies a narrow band of ornamental grasses, framing a thin line of orange gravel. Each of these linear ribbons of plants has the effect of counter-weighting the presence of sculpture. The question that inevitably arises: why asymmetrical? why imbalance? This wonder resonates as we follow the footpath around the rectangular outer edge of the space, through an allée of honey locusts, and along a series of naturalistic perennial gardens. Olin artfully leaves it unanswered.

GARDEN OPEN: 9 am to 5 pm daily. **ADMISSION:** free.

FURTHER INFORMATION FROM:
2400 North Stockton Drive, Chicago 60614
(312) 742-7736

NEARBY SIGHTS OF INTEREST:
Lincoln Park Zoo, Goethe statue, Lake Michigan

2 Chicago: Lincoln Park Conservatory and Gardens

LOCATION: LINCOLN PARK DRIVE AND FULLERTON AVENUE, NORTH SIDE OF THE CITY NEAR LAKE MICHIGAN

The conservatory in Lincoln Park was built in 1892, at the onset of Chicago's economic rise, when the city's financial elite began clamoring for a grand conservatory—that most aristocratic of city accouterments. The structure, designed by Chicago-based architect Joseph Lyman Silsbee, has an industrial cast. Unlike the Garfield Conservatory, little attempt has been made here to hide the engineering of the venerable structure. For instance, views within the palm house typically include the heavy cogs of the louver system or the thick concrete pilings that hold the building up and wear a century of green paint. The Lincoln Park Conservatory is an urban garden that shows its democratic purpose in its lack of pretension.

Yet this is a beautiful garden that has been maintained and renovated over the years. Outside the conservatory lies a belt buckle-shaped depression of sharply defined beds, containing a rich collection of petunias, pansies, and an assortment of annuals and perennials. The idea here is to be as formal as possible, with well-demarcated lines, achieved by an orderly placement of flowers and a vibrant contrast in color. The general architecture of the space is flat, making it difficult to get above the designs in order to look down upon them—the greatest vantage for a garden of this type. A slight verticality is inserted here and there with the use of birds of paradise and palmettos—making connection with the tropical theme of the hothouse.

The conservatory is divided into four rooms, each addressing the theme, developed in the early years of the garden and continued to this day, of presenting tropic plants of the old and new world—namely, Asiatic and American plants. The palm is the tallest room and greets visitors on arrival. A central bed, lined with an irregular buffer of tufa, contains a variety of mature palms and such exotic hardwoods as mahogany. Ferns, camellias, and a restrained use of flowering shrubs fill the middle and lower planes. A single path circumscribes the room and leads in linear sequence through the fern room, the orchid house, and a "show room," in which selections from all these groupings are mixed together to illustrate their use in design. A small pond artfully defined by three solitary thalia sits in the center of the intimate first room, beyond which lies a steppe of gardenias and bananas.

In front of the building is a progression of flower beds, geometrically arranged and planted with annuals, called the *Grandmother's Garden*. The *parti* here is less formal, although the bones of the space are structured. Walking through the grass spaces between the beds, the experience is mostly concerned with the artful groundplane, although some attempt has been made to build a verticality with the plants, including large-frond banana plants and ornamental grasses. Because the space is long and unbroken visually (with the exception of a modest central fountain), the design seems awkward. The conservatory has hosted a garden of evolving styles since the 1890s; what we see today presents a wholly modern feeling.

A skilled garden curator sculpts tropical wonders at the Lincoln Park Conservatory.

3 # Chicago: Garfield Conservatory

GARDEN OPEN: 9 am to 5 pm daily. **ADMISSION:** free.

LOCATION: CORNER OF LAKE STREET AND CENTRAL PARK AVENUE, ON THE SOUTHWEST SIDE OF THE CITY; ACCESSIBLE BY THE GREEN LINE ELEVATED TRAIN

FURTHER INFORMATION FROM:
300 North Central Park
Avenue, Chicago, 60624
(312) 746-5100
www.garfield-conservatory.org

NEARBY SIGHTS OF INTEREST:
Ukrainian National Museum,
Jane Addams House, Maxwell
Street Market

Jens Jensen's prairie style is discernible in this tropical display at the Garfield Conservatory.

Jens Jensen's prairie style is most often associated with larger landscapes, those that match actual prairies in scale and mode. Yet when Jensen designed a new conservatory for Garfield Park as supervisor of the west parks district in Chicago, he created an enclosed tropical garden in keeping with the era's Edwardian fervor for all things exotic. Instead of prairie-style native grasses and hawthorn trees, Jensen applied the same design principles that guided his prairie landscapes but employed them in a tropical setting. The two main rooms of the conservatory offer subtly contrasting approaches. Both are organized around circular walkways, however the first gives the sense of a more traditional palm house, with tall, vertiginous trunks of palm trees swaying high over the neat, concrete path. The plant material is arranged in artful layers of contrasting texture and a uniform pastiche of lush green. Although there is no labeling and the sense is that plant design is favored over horticulture, Jensen's approach is strangely ordered, as if he were self-consciously rejecting the tenets of conservatory design without offering an entirely original conception of the form. In the second main room, Jensen designed a kind of sunken garden, in which the pathway that takes visitors around the displays literally causes them to duck their heads and dodged errant palm fronds. This precursor to what today is called the "immersion experience" in zoo and botanical garden design must have awed Chicagoans at the turn of the century, when it was a shocking experience simply to see these exotic plants—never mind being smacked in the back of the head by one. The gentlest trickle of water fills the utilitarian architecture with a mellow ambiance, while the mature plant collections exhibit visual depth, to the point of seeming almost primeval.

4 Oak Park: Oak Park Conservatory

LOCATION: CORNER OF EAST AVENUE AND GARFIELD STREET, A CLOSE-IN
SUBURB WEST OF THE CITY

But for the grace of Oak Park residents we would not be able to enjoy this conservatory today. The glass structure was built in 1929 and fitted out with exotic specimens gathered by local garden aficionados who returned from their travels with arms brimming with plants. In 1970 the garden fell on hard times and it was almost demolished. A plucky group of Oak Parkians banded together and found the resources to save the building, restore the glass, and keep it open to the public. Three gardens form the backbone to the conservatory. The *Desert House* mixes arid flowers, cacti, and an array of succulents around a circular, ambulating path. At the far end are Biblical plants and a garden of sensory plants, which are particularly good to smell and touch. The *Tropical Garden* is organized around an enormous central fig tree that wears an equally impressive climbing vine of the Aracea family. A fish-filled pond with waterfall in the middle of the room provides a nice trickling effect. At one end is a stone bench overhung by a palm arbor. The *Fern House* is the last room of the main conservatory. A large mound rises in the center of the space, planted over its expanse with a diversity of frondy ferns, including tree ferns. Begonias, orchids, and a collection of bromeliads provide color. At one end lies a bog with carnivorous plants. Outside the conservatory volunteer gardeners have planted perennial gardens that feature flowering prairie varieties. In the near future three new additions—a gazebo, and herb and prairie gardens—will be developed. The garden is well-used by the community, although on a much smaller scale than its counterparts in the city. As such it exudes an informal air, which can often be refreshing.

GARDEN OPEN: 10 am to 5 pm
Monday–Saturday, noon to 5
pm Sunday, year-round; 10
am to 8 pm Friday and
Saturday, June–August.
ADMISSION: free.

FURTHER INFORMATION FROM:
2218 North Prospect Road,
Peoria 61603
(309) 686-3362
www.peoriaparks.org

NEARBY SIGHTS OF INTEREST:
Glen Oak Zoo, Illinois
Historical Water Museum

This small, community-centered conservatory on the west side of the city boasts delightful design features.

GARDEN OPEN: dawn to dusk
daily. ADMISSION: free.

FURTHER INFORMATION FROM:
Northwestern University
Public Relations Department,
Evanston 60201
(847) 864-8384

NEARBY SIGHTS OF INTEREST:
Northwestern University,
Grosse Pointe Lighthouse,
Mitchell Indian Museum

*Formal features, such as this
central path culminating in a
stone exedra, give Jens
Jensen's Shakespeare Garden
structure and focus.*

5 Evanston: Shakespeare Garden

LOCATION: ON THE NORTHWESTERN UNIVERSITY CAMPUS

The Shakespearean Garden on the campus of Northwestern
University is for garden lovers, more than the usual iconoclastic product of a devoted anachronist who relishes the arcana of
Elizabethan England. It was designed and planted in 1915 by
the landscape architect Jens Jensen. As one of the few landscapes by Jensen that has been well-preserved, it holds more
significance as a relic of American landscape architecture than
it does as an homage to Shakespeare. The garden is organized
as an elongated oval, sliced through the middle by a wide, central path of grass. Beds of flowers and herbs line each side of
this axis, plants that are mentioned in the playwright's works.
Among these are woodbine, violet, an abundance of thyme, and
the greenwood tree from *As You Like It*. At one end of the space
sits an exedra, a semicircular bench, against a backdrop of
viburnum, balanced at the other by a bas-relief monument to
the bard. Overlaid on the garden is Jensen's distinctive palette
of native Illinois species, including several mature hawthorns
that give a midwestern context to what has become a common
garden trope.

6 Willmette: Bahai Temple

LOCATION: CORNER OF SHERIDAN ROAD AND LINDEN AVENUE, FIFTEEN MILES NORTH OF CHICAGO

The Bahai faith was born in the nineteenth century when Muslim prophet Baha'u'llah declared that all the monotheistic religions of the world were simply different variations of the same theme, that Christians, Jews, Buddhists, and Muslims all worshipped the same God, just in different ways. Although many of the tenets of Islam make hints in this direction, this prophet's radical holism was too much for the Islamic powers and they labeled him a heretic.

Bahai essentially absorbs all religions into a spiritual system that places the emphasis on spirituality rather than politics. Because of this it has found a following in the United States, with world headquarters for the Bahai located in Willmette, Illinois, an affluent suburban community. The marble temple rising near the shores of Lake Michigan is truly stunning, not only for its majestic presence, but for the fact that every inch of the exterior surface is engraved with the symbolism of the world's religions—crucifixes next to stars of David next to the Hindu symbol of the swastika. Surrounding the temple on each of the eight sides are meticulously organized gardens. Yew hedges partition and segment the space into neat parcels, easily digestible to the eye. A mix of shrubbery occupies each garden section of the temple's edge, while a panel of turf, laced along its edge by vibrant flower beds, radiates outward. The plant palette is exuberant, including a line of evergreen arbor vitae contrasted with a carpet of lavender. In another section one finds the soft, layered composition of native honey locusts underlain with a cover of pachysandra and assorted perennials. The garden has metaphysical significance to the Bahais. According to the central text of the Bahai faith it was in the garden of Ridvan, outside of Baghdad, that Baha'u'llah revealed his mission to his followers. But the idea of the garden as a place of peace and bounty, an idea not unfamiliar to Muslims, peppers much of the theology as well, including specific references to the geometry of the circle and gardens that "radiate" from the center. The literal derivations of this garden may be somewhat tentative, yet its metaphorical and spiritual dimensions remain vivid for any visitor, regardless of faith.

GARDEN OPEN: 10 am to 10 pm daily, May–September; 10 am to 5 pm daily, October–April.
ADMISSION: free.

FURTHER INFORMATION FROM: Bahai House of Worship, Willmette 60091 (847) 853-2300

NEARBY SIGHTS OF INTEREST: Northwestern University, Chicago Botanic Garden

For the B'Hai, the garden symbolizes paradise.

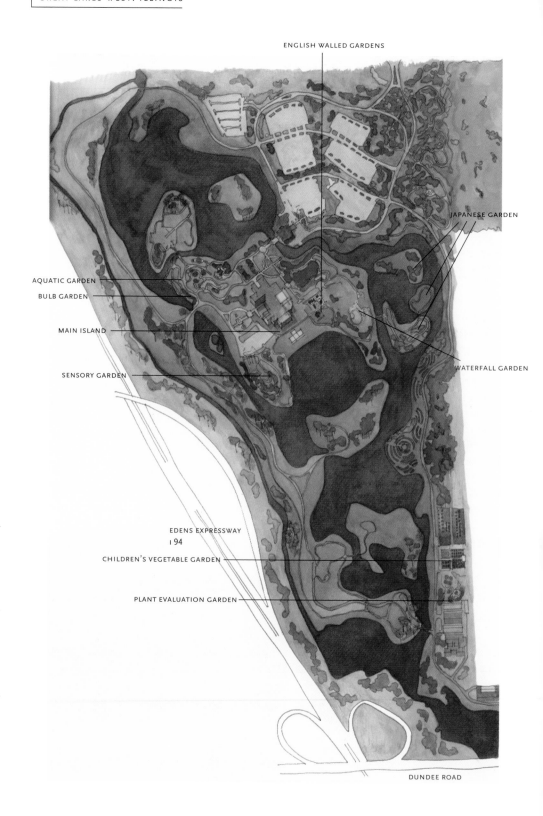

ENGLISH WALLED GARDENS

JAPANESE GARDEN

AQUATIC GARDEN

BULB GARDEN

MAIN ISLAND

SENSORY GARDEN

WATERFALL GARDEN

EDENS EXPRESSWAY
I 94

CHILDREN'S VEGETABLE GARDEN

PLANT EVALUATION GARDEN

DUNDEE ROAD

7 Glencoe: Chicago Botanic Garden

LOCATION: LAKE COOK ROAD, OFF ROUTE 41, TWENTY-FIVE MILES
NORTH OF CHICAGO

GARDEN OPEN: 8 am to sunset
daily, except Christmas.
Admission: free.

FURTHER INFORMATION FROM:
1000 Lake Cook Road
Glencoe 60022
(847) 835-5440
www.chicago-botanic.org

NEARBY SIGHTS OF INTEREST:
Ravinia Music Festival,
Chipilly Woods

In many ways, the spiritual origins of the Chicago Botanic
Garden date back to 1837 when the city fathers adopted the
motto "City in a Garden." The botanic garden was an idea cast
about over many decades by the city's horticultural society,
which believed that Chicago should sport a public garden com-
parable to that found in East Coast cities, but that would showcase the unique flora and vegetation of this region. For many
years it seemed that the city would find a location downtown,
but when momentum finally built in the 1950s, the place along
the marshy lakefront, many miles from the city, was chosen.

When he arrived in 1963 on this lowly spot on the outer
edge of Cook County, Pittsburgh landscape architect John O.
Simonds found a polluted slough called Skokie Lagoon.
Simonds, the son of Chicago garden maker Ossian Cole (O. C.)
Simonds and progenitor, like O.C., of a regional approach to
landscape design—called prairie style earlier in the century—
set about transforming the mosquito-infested moggy bottoms
into arable land by way of a massive program of earthworks.
Instead of simply filling the land, however, Simonds balanced
gently mounded hillocks and a labyrinthine maze of placid
waters into a complex, layered landscape, an aesthetic derived
from the gardens of Suzhou, China. The heart of the garden is
a large island in the middle of the lagoon, upon which rests the
educational center designed by Edward Larrabee Barnes.

*Large midwestern vistas are
found throughout the Chicago
Botanic Garden.*

ABOVE, TOP: *Rustic details, like this simple arbor, create a homey aesthetic.*

ABOVE, CENTER: *The exquisite Japanese garden contains a wealth of sculptural features.*

ABOVE, BOTTOM: *Intimate spaces are carved from the landscape.*

BELOW: *Even the gates are designed with care.*

Emanating from here along a network of pathways that penetrate the 385 acres of the site are a full variety of gardens types, befitting the public education mission of an urban botanical garden, including all the usual suspects: a Japanese garden, a rose garden, plenty of bedded out annuals and perennial borders. But beyond this there are two distinctive spirits guiding the place, each reminiscent of a specific time in garden history. The Chicago Horticultural Society, which administers the botanic garden, has its roots in the 1910s and continues to exhibit a classic Edwardian passion for exotic varieties and unusual hybrids that, at the turn of the twentieth century, sent explorers around the world in pursuit of the newest, most outlandish botanical specimens. One of the Society's emphatic statements was its design of the Horticultural Hall at the World's Colombian Exposition in Chicago in 1893, an outrageous collection of palms and tropical flowers that awed visitors unaccustomed to such sights. Today this confident spirit still guides the botanic garden, notably in the two plant evaluation gardens set off from the main garden area. Here resident botanists test the viability of specimens gathered from abroad. Pragmatism melds with aesthetics, as scientists continue to seek the beautiful and the useful.

The second guiding spirit of the Chicago Botanic Garden is the focus on native plants. To this end the northeast quadrant of the property is given over to the *McDonald Woods*, a 100-acre woodland that is being restored, and another 15 acres maintained as prairie that showcase the native grasses that once completely

covered this region. There is also an *endangered species garden* that is planted with many endangered wildflowers and herbaceous plants lost over the last hundred years.

Situated in between these two spirits—botany's pursuit of the exotic, and ecology's restoration of native landscape—are the gardens proper. These are laid out on the main island and the nearby shores of the lagoon. It is unusual to discover a garden that can tell a story or explain an idea clearly or even literally. The *English Walled Garden* is such a place, where we find six, easily distinguishable English garden types, arrayed to provide an informative narrative about this tradition. Another exquisite place within the garden is *Sansho-En,* the Japanese garden that occupies three small islands in the lagoon. Although the entire botanic garden was conceived along eastern lines, a fact particularly discernible in Simonds' use of the theories of *feng shui* to balance elevations and water, the Japanese garden was designed separately in 1982. Oriented as a strolling garden, Sansho-En features a layered canvas of Asiatic foliage (evergreen mostly) with slight hints of color here and there. The gently rolling landscape is dotted with a few architectural features, such as bridges and small lanterns, to focus views.

The formal gardens offer interesting comparisons. The *Heritage Garden* is derived from the early botanical gardens of Padua, Italy. It is designed in four quadrants with plant families divided accordingly. In contrast, the *Circle Garden* is early American in inspiration, featuring seasonal flowers in a showy display around a central fountain. Winding around all of these is a meadow garden that flows like a ribbon around the main island, growing every year. Aesthetically it seems to nod in both directions, toward the nativistic and ecological realm as well as toward the traditional European-inspired realm of English cottage gardens. In addition to these, there are more educational gardens, such as a home demonstration area, a special-needs garden with raised beds and tactile plants, and a dwarf conifer collection.

A major civic attraction, the Chicago Botanic Garden requires a fair amount of walking to see all the sights. A ramble around the lake is a memorable experience; the prairie and woodland are crucial to understanding the garden, its history, and the natural environment of the Chicago region.

A sea of tulips and a midwestern river complete the varied assemblage.

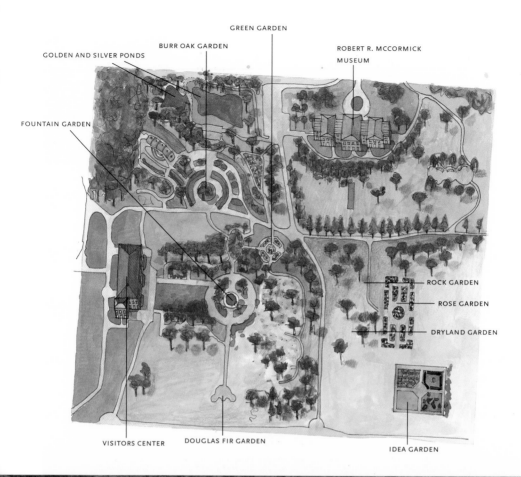

GREEN GARDEN

BURR OAK GARDEN

ROBERT R. McCORMICK
MUSEUM

GOLDEN AND SILVER PONDS

FOUNTAIN GARDEN

ROCK GARDEN

ROSE GARDEN

DRYLAND GARDEN

IDEA GARDEN

VISITORS CENTER

DOUGLAS FIR GARDEN

9 Wheaton: Cantigny

LOCATION: THREE MILES NORTH OF INTERSTATE **88**, AT THE WINFIELD ROAD
EXIT, THIRTY MILES WEST OF CHICAGO

GARDEN OPEN: 9 am to sunset
Tuesday–Sunday,
March–December; 9 am to
sunset Friday–Sunday,
February; closed January and
holidays. **ADMISSION:** free.

FURTHER INFORMATION FROM:
1 South 151 Winfield Road,
Wheaton 60187
(630) 668-5161
www.rrmtf.org/cantigny

NEARBY SIGHTS OF INTEREST:
West Chicago Prairie
Preservation, Cosley Animal
Farm

There was a time when the town of Wheaton was little, when being thirty miles outside of Chicago felt as distant as a hundred miles or a thousand. It was during this time (the 1890s) that the newspaper magnate Joseph Medill, founder of the Chicago Tribune Company, established a 1,500-acre gentleman's farm, Red Oaks, in Wheaton. Medill and his newspaper were staunch Republicans and in decades previous President Lincoln had enjoyed his loyal support when many Illinoisans were beginning to doubt the political impulses of the Illinois-born president. In the twentieth century, Medill's grandson, Robert McCormick, transformed Red Oaks into that curious amalgam of private estate and public gathering place. In 1919 he held a reunion of the U. S. Army's First Division, with which he had served at the battle of Cantigny, the first American victory of World War One. The moment overcame "the Colonel" and he renamed his ancestral estate in their honor.

At his death in 1955 McCormick set Cantigny aside as a public trust and opened the grounds as part museum and part public park. In addition to a First Division museum, there is a golf course, McCormick's mansion (designed by the Boston architect C. A. Coolidge), and ten acres of extraordinary gardens. The gardens were designed in the 1960s and 1970s by Chicago landscape architect Franz Lipp. Lipp's education in horticulture began in the internment camps for German civilians in Australian during World War I. In the 1920s he emigrated from Leipzig and for a brief period studied botany at Harvard University's Arnold Arboretum. As Cantigny shows, Lipp's true genius was his formal design sensibility and talent for combining geometrical spaces to flow from one to another. The gardens begin opposite the austere visitor's center at the entrance. At the end of a grass mall lies the *fountain garden*. A deep green hedge provides a backdrop to a Beaux-Arts fountain that spouts enormous jets of water. An artful arrangement of hydrangeas and other perennials are laid out under a full canopy of spring flowering trees such as magnolias and mature honey locusts that drape the space with dappled light. Each side of the mall has been cultivated as a *scallop garden,* which refers to its shape. On the north side are shade-loving annuals and perennials, while on the south are tuberous flowers such as begonias. To the south of the fountain garden is a small but eclectic collection of native and exotic trees, screened from

OPPOSITE: *In the last 20 years the estate of* Chicago Tribune *publishing magnate Robert McCormick has been developed into wondrous gardens.*

BELOW: *Precious touches give the gardens a candy taste.*

the formal gardens by a single layer of woodland. Among the varieties are an association of ash and flowering dogwood, bur oaks, larches, and the European-inspired silver maples and weeping beeches. Woven into these informal collections are two naturalistic gardens: a *rock garden*, featuring creeping juniper that lies atop an assortment of local stone, and a *dry garden*.

The formal gardens lie to the north of this area, and are accessed from the visitor's center by proceeding down a narrow paved path that is lined by American linden, euonymus, and a delicate bed overflowing with impatiens. The *Bur Oak Garden*, located at the end of this pleasant little allée, provides Cantigny with its stock of postcard shots. The small bur oak in the middle of the garden replaces a centenarian stalwart that finally died in 1990. Other permanent fixtures include a radial arrangement of hawthorns anchoring the flowerbeds, and a surround of lilac and arborvitae hedge that separate this room from the rest of the garden. The floral display changes every year and through the seasons, with the one constant—designed by Lipp and his successors at Cantigny—of a visually bold and breathtaking display. The design philosophy is closely aligned with the "new American garden" style advocated by the Washington, D.C., garden designers Oehme Van Sweden. Like Wolfgang Oehme, Franz Lipp was educated in the classical horticultural colleges of Germany and brought to Cantigny a sen-

The display gardens, depicted in each of these photos, combine a classical sense for form and texture with a distinctly midwestern plant vocabulary.

sual sense of floral arrangement. Wide swaths of color—impatiens and begonias mixed with grasses and other selections taken from a large horticultural lexicon—are laid side by side in a rich pastiche so that one looks less at individual plants than at the overall composition. Views are manipulated and controlled by the arrangement of beds in rows that radiate from the center and also by topiary cherry trees, trimmed to look like bells, which are places as focal points throughout. Just beyond the confines of the lilac hedge lies a close cousin to the *Bur Oak Garden*: the *Octagonal Garden*. This open space provides a canvas for a constantly evolving display that presses toward the more inventive scale. It is not uncommon to see vegetables,

such as kale or Russian cabbage, interspersed with ornamental grasses and flowers to achieve a visual presentation that is both colorful and textural. Encompassing all of these gardens is a pathway, lined by an iron fence. Set within a series of apses are statuary depicting the four seasons, adorned with vines and small flowers.

The rear face of the mansion, closest to the gardens, is defined by a colonnade of silver maples that replaced an allée of American elms. On the other side of this axis are two newer gardens: an enormous selection of roses and the inventive *Idea Garden*. This last area evolved from the original vegetable garden on-site. Maintained by volunteers, the garden offers gardeners tips on cultivating an herb garden, growing flowers, using containers, and engaging children in botanical pursuits. The tenor of the gardens quiets on the eastern face of the mansion where Lipp designed a memorial landscape for McCormick. Set atop a series of water terraces is a copse of pin oaks enclosing a blue stone plaza and sweeping exedra. McCormick meant for Cantigny to delight and educate the public as much as he meant it to memorialize himself and his grandfather. In some ways this last, most obviously memorial garden, is only a culmination of an idea that threads the entire landscape, including the museums, together.

Franz Lipp possessed a profound understanding of spatial relationships and took care to arrange the gardens as an unfolding experience.

GARDEN OPEN: 7 am to 7 pm daily, during daylight savings time; 7 am to 5 pm the rest of the year. **ADMISSION:** $7 per car; $3 on Wednesday.

FURTHER INFORMATION FROM:
4100 Illinois Route 53,
Lisle 60532-1293
(630) 719-2400
www.mortonarb.org

NEARBY SITES OF INTEREST:
Argonne National Laboratory,
Cantigny

Fabulous fall color at the Morton Arboretum

8   Lisle: Morton Arboretum

LOCATION: ROUTE 53, OFF INTERSTATE 88, TWENTY-FIVE MILES WEST OF CHICAGO

Botanist and founder of the Arnold Arboretum in Boston, Charles Sprague Sargent, wrote of his intent in a 1925 letter just before his death to his new friend Joy Morton in Chicago. Sargent had been helping Morton establish a large arboretum on the west side of city, and, he wrote, "You realize, I hope, that you will be remembered for the Arboretum long after the salt business is forgotten." Indeed, although we have not forgotten Morton Salt, the Morton Arboretum has grown into a significant research institution and public garden. It encompasses 1,700 acres in an area that has been overwhelmed by suburban development in the last twenty years. But in the 1920s when Joy Morton began to transform his Thornhill estate into a "museum of trees," this area was little more than dusty roads speckled with country places of such individualists as Morton. Morton reportedly inherited his interest in trees from his father, Julius Sterling Morton, who served as a secretary of agriculture under Grover Cleveland and was the originator of arbor day. In 1876 Joy and his father journeyed to Boston to celebrate the centennial; during their stay they visited the world-renowned Arnold Arboretum and met Sargent.

Like the Arnold Arboretum, the Morton Arboretum has sought to bring together into one garden a selection of hardy trees that will survive in the northern Illinois climate.

Traditionally this has taken the arborists far afield to places in Asia where an Illinois-like environment has promulgated a pantheon of resilient trees. In recent years native North American species have become a major presence, and the garden includes several areas devoted to specific geographical regions such as Appalachia, the Ozarks, and Illinois. There is probably no finer collection of buckeyes around. In the far western corner of the garden is the *Shulenberg Prairie*, a mature restored landscape featuring tall grasses and colorful flowers in the summer and autumn. Besides trees there are several areas of naturalized flowers and an area of horticultural collections, consisting mostly of hedges and groundcover, located near to the library and research facilities. Set as a backdrop to these formal areas are the *Four Columns*, an architectural focal point erected by Sterling Morton, Joy's son, during his tenure as arboretum director in the 1950s. A fragrance garden in this area exhibits an assortment of vines, shrubs, and flowers arranged around a lotus-filled pool and shaded arbor seat.

One of the best ways to see the entire arboretum is by tram bus, a feature in the garden since 1937. Knowledgeable docents give a thorough introduction to the mission of the institution and its collections. Afterwards, if time permits, sojourn to the Sterling Library and the *May T. Watts Reading Garden*, to enjoy one of the unusual volumes among the serene scene of this small, quiet place.

10 Rockford: Klehm Arboretum

LOCATION: CLIFTON STREET, OFF MAIN STREET, TWO MILES NORTH OF STATE HIGHWAY 2

In the realm of landscape, nursery people are often the most experimental. According to theories of capitalism, they should be: the better plants they grow, the better business they will do. Often this experimentation can take on creative and artistic tones, such as with William Lincoln Taylor, proprietor of the Rockford Nursery, which beginning in 1910 kept this northern Illinois city in rare trees. The Klehm family purchased the site in 1968 and donated it to the local forest preserve district in the 1980s. The Klehms added to Taylor's work, and today the arboretum contains one of the most unusual collections of trees in the country. Among the native species and exotics, there is an extensive and vigorous collection of evergreens, including Chamaecyparis, junipers, spruces, pines, Douglas firs, yews, arborvitae, and hemlock, as well as a bur oak collection, the largest of which are over 300 years old. Beneath their canopy is a collection of umbrella magnolias, an unusual specimen to find in this climate. There

GARDEN OPEN: 9 am to 4 pm daily, year-round; open until 8 pm Monday, June–August . ADMISSION: $2.

FURTHER INFORMATION FROM: 1220 Rock Street, Rockford 61101 (815) 965-8146 www.klehm.org

NEARBY SIGHTS OF INTEREST: Tinker Swiss Cottage Museum, Riverfront Museum Park

*A perennial walk
complements a diverse
collection of trees at the Klehm
Arboretum.*

are several truly rare species in the collection including the spiny Hemiptelea from northern China and Fontanesia, a willow-like plant of the olive family.

The arboretum also contains several formal garden areas, including the *Fountain Garden*. Curving walkways wind through an amorphous space, defined by raised border gardens of perennials and herbaceous grasses. In addition to the fountain there is a gazebo and several trellises. There are also several demonstration gardens, including the *Butterfly Garden*, the *Everlasting Garden* of flowers that can be dried, and the *Square Food Garden*, a container garden that reportedly uses only twenty percent of the space to produce the same amount of vegetables as a conventional row garden. In fall months, particular favorites include the *Gourd Garden* and the *Prehistoric Garden*, which contains ferns, mosses, and ginkgoes that fossil records indicate have existed since the Mesozoic.

11 Rockford: Anderson Gardens

LOCATION: PARKVIEW AVENUE AND SPRING CREEK, EAST OF THE ROCK RIVER, ON THE SOUTH SIDE OF THE CITY

GARDEN OPEN: 10 am to 4 pm Monday–Saturday, May–October; 10 am to 8 pm Thursday–Saturday, June–August. **ADMISSION:** $4 adults, $3 seniors, $2 students 5–18 years, free on the third Thursday of the month.

FURTHER INFORMATION FROM:
340 Spring Creek Road,
Rockford 61107-1035
(815) 229-9390

NEARBY SIGHTS OF INTEREST:
Tinker Swiss Cottage, Midway Village and Museum

Illinois businessman John Anderson found himself in Portland, Oregon, with nothing to do one day in the early 1970s and asked a taxi driver for recommendations. The driver took Anderson up to Washington Park, where, besides wonderful views of the city and surrounding countryside, he visited one of the best Japanese gardens in the country. Anderson returned to Rockford intent on developing a place of equal value. Hoichi Kurisu, a past director of the Portland garden, designed the Anderson gardens in 1978. Located on five acres, the gardens present several different traditions at once. Just inside the entrance is a large pond with several small islands. An array of architectural features, such as a pagoda, small stone lanterns, and bamboo bridges, train the eye upon the landscape. A walking path takes visitors around the perimeter of the pond. As it weaves through the garden it also forces views and modulates one's experience. This controlled design is in the style of the Kamakura period (1185–1333 AD). An emphasis on peace pervades the garden. At an early bend in the path, stepping stones gracefully cross a stream, while a waterfall fills the air with a gentle, rushing sound. Further along is a viewing house built at the edge of the pond where visitors are encouraged to relax and meditate in silence.

At the far end of the pond is the *ZigZag* bridge, a wooden breezeway designed in a sharp, jagged manner. In Japanese tradition evil spirits travel in straight lines, thus falling in the water if they were to pursue you through this area. At the conclusion of the walking path is a handsome, restrained guest house, designed in the Sukiya style for the tea ceremony. Although off-limits to garden visitors, it provides an architectural backdrop to the dry garden style, the second major style, found in the small formal garden next to the guest house. Here are beds of raked gravel and carefully placed boulders. In some literal expressions (and interpretations) this design is meant to convey a sense of oceans and islands, with the gravel being the water; however here, perhaps because of its juxtaposition against several other garden designs, the dry garden is simply a beautiful component in a larger array of ideas. Uphill from here is a tea house and gazebo, situated around a quiet viewing garden dominated by moss, cryptomeria, and the more pronounced gush of a large waterfall and stream. Because the house, designed by noted Japanese designer Masahiro Hamada, is meant for the sacred tea ceremony, the gardens have been arranged in the viewing style. A path winds around the stream, carrying visitors close to the waterfall, yet this space is meant for silent sitting and watching, even hours of studying a single spot.

A modern visitor center is built outside the confines of the garden and offers an array of public education programs about the beauty of Japanese gardening traditions.

Inspired by his travels to the Far East, Rockford businessman John Anderson built this fine Japanese garden.

12 Rock Island: Quad City Botanical Center

LOCATION: FOURTH AVENUE, ALONG THE RIVER, DOWNTOWN

Twelve years in the making, the Quad City Botanical Center opened in 1998. Although outdoor gardens take a long time to mature, enclosed conservatories benefit at the beginning from design and plant donations. The structure was designed by Change Environmental Architecture of Cedar Rapids, Iowa, and represents a new approach to glasshouses. Instead of a dome, the building is jewel-like, with levels of glass rising up squarely. This allows excessive heat in summer months to be easily vented off. The east and west faces of the building are insulated to prevent radical shifts in temperature during summer and winter. The landscape design, executed by Thomas Graceffa of Rockford, is also innovative. Graceffa worked off the cornucopia shape of the ground plane to segregate tall plants like palms and create a layered mixture of overstory and understory trees. The collections were bolstered recently by the anonymous donation of 85 Hawaiian bromeliads—prickly, cupped plants of which the pineapple is the best known. The garden also features orchids, ferns, and the usual display of tropicals, such as lemon trees, coffee plants, and many different kinds of palms. A reflective pool at the southern end of the conservatory extends outside the structure where a small, relaxing conifer garden has been planted. The garden is in its infancy, and educational events, flower displays, and other programs are just getting underway.

13 Moline: Butterworth Center and Deere-Wiman House

LOCATION: CORNER OF 8TH STREET AND 11TH AVENUE, DOWNTOWN

John Deere revolutionized farming in 1837 when he invented a steel plow that enabled Midwestern farmers to turn prairie into agricultural land. His son, Charles Deere, revolutionized Moline, Illinois, when he built a magnificent mansion there in 1870. The architect was William Le Baron Jenny; the landscape architect is unknown, although it was not unusual for the architect to design the grounds. Today there are three well-tended, Victorian style rose gardens. Fountains, brick terraces, and artful displays of old-fashioned roses mixed with perennials give the gardens life through the summer. A slight grade change, and the steps and pathways that accommodate this, give the gardens definition. In 1892 the Deeres built another house nearby for their daughter. It was called Hillcrest at the time, though when Katherine Deere Butterworth bequeathed the house and an ornate garden to a public trust she named it Butterworth Center. One side is lined with a long, white trellis covered with climbing roses; the other is lined with a pergola sheltering a quiet terrace. The interior of the garden is designed as rows and rectangles of perennials, designed in the cottage garden style in large swaths of color. The lines and composition retain their old world grandeur, while the horticultural treatment bespeaks a modern interpretation—heirloom plants are combined with hostas and spring bulbs. The house is maintained as a period museum, including an immense organ dating to 1909.

GARDEN OPEN: Dawn to dusk daily, year-round.
ADMISSION: free.
HOUSE OPEN: Monday–Friday by appointment.
TOURS: 1 pm to 4 pm on the hour Sundays, July and August. ADMISSION: free.

FURTHER INFORMATION FROM: 1105 8th Street, Moline 61265
(309) 765-7971

NEARBY SIGHTS OF INTEREST: Deere and Company, Rock Island Arsenal

OPPOSITE, TOP: *Hothouse botanicals.*

OPPOSITE, BOTTOM: *A new jewel-like conservatory graces the Quad Cities.*

14 Peoria: George L. Luthy Memorial Botanical Garden

LOCATION: CORNER OF PROSPECT ROAD AND MCCLURE, IN GLEN OAK PARK, ON THE WESTERN BANK OF THE ILLINOIS RIVER, SOUTH OF HIGHWAY 150

Glen Oak Park used to sport one of the most impressive Victorian glass houses in the country. But like most conservatories, this one deteriorated over the years, and in 1951 a new, modern structure went up in its place. One of the garden's directors, George Luthy, was a consummate rosarian, and he planted an impressive collection of roses before the new conservatory, which would eventually receive All-America designation. The garden was named after Luthy in the 1970s, and has grown significantly since then.

Some of the plants in the conservatory are old palms rescued from the original glasshouse, today mixed in with a full

GARDEN OPEN: noon to 4 pm Monday–Friday; noon to 5 pm Saturday and Sunday; closed on Christmas Eve and Christmas. ADMISSION: free.

FURTHER INFORMATION FROM: P.O. Box 5052, Springfield 62705
(217) 753-6228

NEARBY SIGHTS OF INTEREST: Lincoln Home, Lincoln Tomb, Lincoln Memorial Gardens

selection of tropicals. The rose garden remains well-tended, and with 900 roses it is a big attraction. Around the grounds are various small specialty themes of various quality and type. One of the most interesting, at least in the near future, will be the *Wilson Garden*. Originally this had been a sunken garden located at the far end of Glen Oak Park, which was named for the plant explorer Earnest Wilson in 1932 after he died tragically in a car accident. The garden was moved here in the 1950s, and continued to be tended by the Wilson Society. As a general flower garden in which the color purple (a favorite of a society member) predominates, the garden has never really honored Wilson, who discovered over 1,200 different species of exotic plants. An effort has recently been undertaken to add some of these species to the mix.

Elsewhere is an attractive lawn hemmed in by flowering crabapples, many of which date back to the 1930s. There is also a rectangular cottage garden, with a curving brick-lined rubber tree in the middle. Here, drifts of perennials mix with a restrained vocabulary of understory trees, including Carolina silverbell and weeping cherry. The *Herb Garden* features a sundial, original to the park that dates to 1905 as well as old timey herbs. A dwarf conifer was recently added to the gardens and has quickly become one of the most popular places. The plants are arranged on a single mound, in order to bring smaller varieties up to eye level.

The Lincoln Memorial Garden is also meant to express the midwestern character.

Located in a public park, the garden has a strong civic presence. A newly opened children's garden has been coordinated with a local abuse counseling center. A maze and various plant areas are used as part of a horticultural therapy program.

15 Springfield: Lincoln Memorial Garden

LOCATION: EAST LAKE DRIVE AND PAWNEE ROAD, ON LAKE SPRINGFIELD

GARDEN OPEN: Dawn to dusk daily, year-round.

ADMISSION: free.

NATURE CENTER OPEN: 10 am to 4 pm Tuesday–Saturday, 1 pm to 4 pm Sundays.

FURTHER INFORMATION FROM:
2301 East Lake Shore Drive, Springfield 62707
(217) 529-1111

NEARBY SIGHTS OF INTEREST:
Henson Robinson Zoo, Lincoln Home National Historic Site

Jens Jensen's extant masterpiece in Springfield is a memorial to President Abraham Lincoln.

Although they never knew each other, Abraham Lincoln might well have admired Jens Jensen. Like many of the soldiers that fought in the Civil War from Lincoln's home state of Illinois, Jensen was an immigrant. He also possessed a clear and noble vision of democracy as perhaps the greatest activity of a civilization. These are strange things to say about a landscape architect, yet there was little typical in Jensen.

Jensen's best preserved work is this 77-acre homage to Lincoln, designed and constructed in his hometown of Springfield, Illinois, where he lived before moving to Washington, D.C., as president in 1861. The garden, a "living memorial" to Lincoln, was the brainchild of Mrs. Harriet Knudson, a member of the local garden club. Knudson contacted Jensen, who by 1936 was an internationally known landscape architect, whose prairie style design was being taught in schools. Jensen's plan for the garden was to replicate, through plant vocabulary and design, the native landscapes of Illinois, Indiana, and northern Kentucky where Lincoln had lived. The path system is organized as a series of parallel veins that move perpendicular to the lake, thus frequently culminating in wonderfully framed views of the water. In addition to a strong palette of trees, Jensen used prairie wildflowers to create colorful effects throughout the seasons. In spring months the woodland is alive with trillium and bluebells; in summer the meadows turn with coneflower, prairie rose, and Kansas gayfeather; and autumn culminates with goldenrod and asters. Placed throughout the garden are eight "council rings," low, circles of stones that are a hallmark of Jensen's designs. Derived from local Indian customs, Jensen's council ring was intended to provide a quiet gathering place. Because of the circular construction no one speaker could be privileged over another, the council ring epitomizing equality in democratic exchange. A local nonprofit group now manages the garden and educational programs. In 1995 an adjacent farm was donated, which is currently being restored to native prairie.

GARDEN OPEN: noon to 4 pm
Monday–Friday; noon to 5 pm
Saturday and Sunday; closed
on Christmas Eve and
Christmas. ADMISSION: free.

FURTHER INFORMATION FROM:
P.O. Box 5052,
Springfield 62705
(217) 753-6228

NEARBY SIGHTS OF INTEREST:
Lincoln Home, Lincoln Tomb,
Lincoln Memorial Gardens

16 Springfield: Washington Park Botanical Garden

LOCATION: IN WASHINGTON PARK, CORNER OF FAYETTE AND CHATHAM ROADS, DOWNTOWN

Springfield's Washington Park was designed and built at the turn of the century, a time when small but important midwestern cities were beginning to develop such significant municipal institutions as libraries, museums, and public parks. Ossian Cole (O. C.) Simonds, a landscape architect from Chicago, was hired to design the park. Simonds' prairie style incorporated native trees, such as sugar maple and yellowwood, in a naturalistic design of rolling meadows and woodlands. Set in the far corner of the park was a little greenhouse, built in 1902 to cultivate plants for the park. Soon the greenhouse became the locus for gardening activities in Springfield, and over the century it has grown into one of the better display gardens for local flora. The small modern conservatory houses tropicals arranged in a rain forest display, much like the Garfield Conservatory in Chicago—although this structure is much smaller. Several oddities are included in this collection, such as a number of carnivorous plants. The main attractions are outdoors, notably the formal rose garden, planted in 1962 and designed by Robert Lawson, a landscape architect who then ran the Springfield parks and recreation department. The Central Illinois Rose Society maintains a strong interest in the collection, and it is wonderfully cared for. Nearby the conservatory is a small Italianate garden with free-standing Ionic columns salvaged from the Lincoln Library at one end and a rectangular wading pool of lilies in the center; it is surrounded by an over-abundance of bright annuals that spill out of stone planters. A major attraction is the monocot, or single seed plant garden, which features a spectacular assemblage of irises, lilies, and daylilies. It is also overseen by a local garden society. Finishing out the collections are a cactus garden, a rock garden, bonsai kept within the conservatory, a shade garden of hostas and ferns underplanted with colorful impatiens, and an informally mixed perennial border garden to give the home garden ideas. Over the years the Washington Park Botanical Garden has been singled out as one of the better-maintained gardens in the country, which for the garden enthusiast makes for a splendid visit.

17 Indianapolis: Garfield Park Conservatory and Sunken Gardens

LOCATION: CORNER OF RAYMOND STREET AND GARFIELD SOUTH DRIVE, SOUTH SIDE OF THE CITY

In the early decades of the twentieth century the south side of Indianapolis was known as the garden center of the state. Greenhouses marked many of the blocks and grew flowers that were shipped all over the country. Garfield Park was an open space, known by various names until settling on the present one in 1881, after the assassination of President James Garfield. The modern aluminum conservatory was built in the 1950s and renovated in the 1990s. The displays of tropical rainforest are arranged as a walking tour of the Amazonian basin, featuring such plants as trumpet tree, mahogany, various fruits, and a selection of palms. The single, circuitous path winds around a central 15-foot waterfall. A gazebo room hosts an ever-revolving flower show, the highlight of which is the chrysanthemum show in the fall, a mainstay since 1947. Outside the conservatory are the *Sunken Gardens*, originally designed and planted in 1916. After a major restoration the gardens have been returned to their original splendor (albeit they could use several more years of growing). The design is Victorian in inspiration, with majestic brick groundscape designs and ornate fountains. In recent years the conservatory has geared itself toward children. An "explorer scavenger hunt" has been instituted to keep them occupied.

GARDEN OPEN: 10 am to 8 pm Monday–Friday; 10 am to 6 pm Saturday and Sunday, May–October; 10 am to 6 pm daily, November–April.
ADMISSION: $2.00 adults, $1.50 seniors, $1.00 children 4–17 years.

FURTHER INFORMATION FROM: 2505 Conservatory Drive, Indianapolis 46203 (317) 327-7184

NEARBY SIGHTS OF INTEREST: Eiteljorg Museum, Indiana State Museum

The venerable Garfield Park Conservatory has received new life.

GARDEN OPEN: 10:00 am to 5:00 pm Tuesday–Saturday, noon to 5:00 pm Sundays; closes at 8:30 pm on Thursday. **ADMISSION:** free.

FURTHER INFORMATION FROM:
1200 West 38th Street,
Indianapolis 46208-4196
(317) 923-1331
www.ima-art.org

NEARBY SIGHTS OF INTEREST:
Eiteljorg Museum of
American Indians and
Western Art

The formal gardens of the Indianapolis Museum of Art complement a classic picturesque landscape.

18 Indianapolis:
Indianapolis Museum of Art

LOCATION: CORNER OF MICHIGAN ROAD AND WEST 38TH STREET, FIFTEEN MINUTES NORTHWEST OF DOWNTOWN

The Indianapolis Museum of Art contains many significant works of visual art, but none may equal, at least in grandeur, the historic manor located on the grounds. It was built in the 1910s by Hugh McKenna Landon, during the so-called country place era, a time when wealthy Americans began moving out of the cities and constructing palatial residences in the country. Although now enclosed by the city, Oldfields, as the estate was called, was surrounded by woods in the 1920s when Landon hired Percival Gallagher, a young landscape architect with the Olmsted Brothers, to design the landscape. An intelligent designer, Gallagher was impressed by the natural beauty of the site, which included a precipitous grade change of more than fifty feet. This provided the canvas for the *Ravine Garden,* a dramatic limestone-lined canal engulfed by flowering bulbs. The architectural inspiration for the design was probably the ravine in Brooklyn's Prospect Park, created by Gallagher's mentor, Frederick Law Olmsted. But here that statement is made within the constraints of residential scale, meaning that it is warm and immediately understandable within the context of the house

and its location near the city. Gallagher also designed an informal border garden. In terms of its bold use of colors and its warm presentation, this garden makes obvious overtures to the English cottage style, rapidly coming into vogue in the U.S. in the 1910s and 1920. Yet the garden lacks the geometric structure so critical to that aesthetic, instead featuring an American interpretation of meandering paths and curving beds. There is also an oversized allée, reminiscent of English designs, that culminates in a fountain and the *Wood Formal Garden*, a Victorian style flower garden organized in highly geometric beds, and enclosed by limestone walls and plenty of aromatic boxwood hedge. In recent years the museum has recommitted itself to the grounds, initiating a connection with a local greenway trail, along which outdoor sculpture is placed, and creating a sensory garden that features plants with unusual textures and smells oriented around a touchable bronze by the artist Pablo Serrano. The *Ravine Garden* has also undergone a massive restoration, which enables us fully to enjoy this significant American garden landscape.

19 Fort Wayne: Headwaters Park

LOCATION: SUPERIOR AND CLINTON STREETS, WHERE THE MAUMEE, ST. JOSEPH, AND ST. MARY'S RIVERS MEET

GARDEN OPEN: daily, year-round. ADMISSION: free.

FURTHER INFORMATION FROM:
Fort Wayne Visitor's Center
1021 South Calhoun Street,
Fort Wayne 46802
(219) 424-3700
www.fwcvb.org

NEARBY SIGHTS OF INTEREST:
Museum of Art, Performing
Arts Center

For years the Maumee and St. Joseph Rivers, which meet in the middle of town to form St. Mary's River, have ritually filled downtown Fort Wayne with muddy waters during the spring floods. A certain bend in the river, a sharp sweep around an asphalt parking lot was particularly susceptible. Several years ago the city commissioned Fort Wayne-born architect Eric Kuhne to replace the parking lot with a park that would mitigate flooding at the same time it gave downtown Fort Wayne a unified center and gathering place. Headwaters Park successfully does both. Smart landscape architecture, such as a curved levee or overlook, provides places for water to go during heavy rains, while formal esplanades, bedded annuals, and native plant walks offer a variety of garden experiences in the middle of the city.

GARDEN OPEN: 10 am to 5 pm
Monday–Saturday, noon to 4
pm Sundays, year-round.
ADMISSION: $3.00 adults,
$1.50 children 4–14 years.

FURTHER INFORMATION FROM:
1100 South Calhoun Street,
Fort Wayne 46802
(219) 427-6440

NEARBY SIGHTS OF INTEREST:
Firefighter's Museum,
Lincoln Museum

*Intimate details, such as this
statuary, complement a
diverse horticultural collection
and educational programs.*

20 Fort Wayne: Foellinger-Freimann Botanical Conservatory

LOCATION: CORNER OF JEFFERSON BOULEVARD AND CALHOUN STREET, DOWNTOWN

An unpretentious trio of greenhouses symbolize the garden culture of Fort Wayne, a delightful medium-sized city that has gone through some tough economic times in recent decades. Helen Foellinger, the publisher of the local newspaper, and attorney William Sowers came up with the idea of the greenhouses in 1983. After a decade, the Freimann Charitable Trust donated $5 million to renovate and expand the gardens, thus bequeathing the hyphenated Foellinger-Freimann name. The conservatory is laid out as three successive gardens, beginning with the *Show House*. Here the garden staff creates six floral displays each year: azaleas and hydrangeas (January–March), tulips and daffodils (March–April), bedded-out annuals in two iterations (April–June and July–September), mums (October–November), and poinsettias during the Christmas season. A trapezoidal-shaped path runs the circuit within this square building, giving views of the gardens on each side. At one bend in the path is a large loquat tree (*Eriobotrya japonica*). The second greenhouse contains a permanent display of tropicals. A pond and waterfall provide structure to a narrative of orchids, palms, and fruit trees, which are each separated like episodes. The last of the linked houses features desert plants. The small circular path is lined by cacti and succulents typically found in the American Sonorran Desert. In 1996 a new entrance garden was added that overflows with perennials in the summer.

21 Columbus: Irwin Home and Gardens

LOCATION: 5TH STREET, BETWEEN LAFAYETTE AND PEARL STREETS, NEAR THE LIBRARY, DOWNTOWN

GARDEN OPEN: 8 am to 4 pm Saturday and Sunday, mid-April–November. **ADMISSION:** free.

FURTHER INFORMATION FROM: Columbus Visitor Center, 506 Fifth Street, Columbus, 47201 (812) 378-2622

NEARBY SIGHTS OF INTEREST: I.M Pei Library, Brown County Museum

For over one hundred years the Irwin family dominated this block in the quiet metropolis of Columbus, located about thirty-five miles south of Indianapolis. The main factor in their presence has remained the Italianate residence built in 1850 by Joseph I. Irwin; a subsequent generation radically expanded it in 1910 and hired Boston architect Henry Phillips to do the work—including the design of a multi-roomed Italian garden. The Irwins still live in the house, which is private, but open their gardens to visitors on summer weekends.

We enter the gardens through an ornate wrought-iron fence, and under the graceful canopy of shade trees. The first room contains a wishing well. Though waterless, the architectural feature lends a focus to the structured square of brick walking paths, lined with boxed hedges. From here, following a short transverse axis through the site, the path leads to a narrow pool, in the center of which rests a delightful, water-spouting cherub. Each end of the pool is kept in tulips during the spring, while stone pots around the edge help balance and define the space. Up a few steps is a semicircular terrace constructed of brick and hedges. In the center sits a playful elephant sculpture. In the background is a wonderfully simple

The Irwin family graciously opens its lovely Italian garden to the public on select days.

grass courtyard, rounded along its far edge by a curved brick wall, which has the effect of cupping and enclosing the entire space. The view, when taken from the wishing well, or the narrow pool, or anywhere along this cross axis, is of layers of space that imbed into one another—cups capping stems, axes interconnecting nodes, and a generally open feeling that allows you to read successive rooms at once.

The main axis of the garden (perpendicular to this transverse) runs from the windowed living room to a tea house. A rectangular grass terrace marks the transition from the house to the garden. This is perhaps the most traditional Italian garden here, featuring flanking pergolas covered in ancient wisteria (some believe dating back to 1910). A brick pathway, lined with a monochromatic tulip border, outlines the space, while two circular pools lying before the pergolas, provide balance. Overlooking the scene from the porches of the house are the busts of Socrates, Diogenes, Plato, and Aristotle, reproductions of those at Hadrian's Villa at Tivoli, outside of Rome. The far end of the garden culminates in a series of limestone steps ascending to a large tea house. The views from here allow the garden design to unfold in a dynamic way, while the shelter provides an enlightened space where one can enjoy the finer things in life.

One assumes that gardens as refined as these require a certain elevation of spirit. That the Irwin family makes them available to the public, surely with some expenditure of their own privacy, only confirms such suspicions.

22 Muncie: Oakhurst Gardens

LOCATION: MINNETRISTA PARKWAY AND WHEELING AVENUE, AT A BEND IN THE WHITE RIVER, DOWNTOWN

GARDEN OPEN: 10 am to 5 pm Tuesday–Saturday, 1 pm to 5 pm Sunday. **ADMISSION:** varies with events and seasons.

FURTHER INFORMATION: 600 West Minnetrista Boulevard, Muncie 47303-2992 (765) 741-5113

NEARBY SIGHTS OF INTEREST: Spiritualist Camp

The Ball family began settling in Muncie in the early nineteenth century. They have left their mark on this town ever since. Ball canning jars and Ball State University may be the best known nationally. Within Muncie proper the Ball estates, a collection of notable mansions congregated on the shores of the White River, are the most visible. Oakhurst, the shingled Victorian home of George Ball, family patriarch, is the aesthetic epicenter of the precinct. Ball's daughter, Elizabeth, graduated from Vassar with a degree in botany, and when she returned to the estate she proceeded with her mother to develop the existing gardens into a sumptuous landscape. What we see today is a restoration based upon photographs that date to the 1930s. Recent additions aim to make the gardens more appealing to a broader audience. These include a new children's garden and a six-acre woodlands and prairie garden. Immediately surrounding the house are lovely formal gardens with a Victorian air. The *Courtyard Garden* is designed with brick and hardscape, softened over the years by an plantings of bulbs and woody plants arranged in the turn-of-the-century cottage style made popular by Gertrude Jekyll and William Robinson. Nestled into the woods at the entrance is the colonnade, Federalist style remnants of an early Ball mansion lined with brick and stone terracing and interspersed with an artful placement of bulbs. Deep in the woods is the Italian influenced *Sunken Garden*, designed in the round. Elizabeth became increasingly preoccupied with the woodlands over time, imagining that they harbored a population of nymphs and fairies. She cultivated a vibrant garden of wildflowers beneath the canopy, and in spring large swaths of blue and yellow over take the grounds. The Oakhurst Gardens are now part of a larger cultural center, host to programs and educational events for local gardeners throughout the year, as well as musical and theatrical programs, including the annual "Midsummer Night's Luminaria Walk" in July when Elizabeth's nymphs come to life.

A lily pond in a sea of bluebells connotes a sense of taste without frivolity at the Oakhurst Gardens.

1   Milwaukee: Boerner Botanical Gardens

2   Milwaukee: Mitchell Park Conservatory

3   Green Bay: Green Bay Botanical Garden

4   Oshkosh: Paine Art Center

5   Madison: Allen Centennial Garden

6   Madison: Olbrich Botanical Gardens

7   Janesville: Rotary Gardens

8   Saint Paul: Como Park Conservatory

9   Chanhassen: Minnesota Landscape Arboretum

10   Wayzata: Noernberg Gardens

11   Duluth: Glensheen and the Duluth Rose Garden

UPPER MIDWEST:

Wisconsin, Minnesota

T wo-thousand years ago the glaciers released their grip on North America and retreated. West of the Great Lakes they left behind a scoured landscape of innumerable small lakes and low, elongated rises, called drumlins. This glacial topography gives Wisconsin and Minnesota one of the most visually enticing landscapes in the Midwest. Long vistas across generally flat lands are given texture by slight undulations; as the eye casts across open space it alights on significant features—an outcrop there, a depression here.

The Minnesota Landscape Arboretum takes full advantage of this condition. It is designed upon the land so that the visitor experiences not only the wonderful collections of the arboretum and intelligent compositions of the formal gardens, but also the larger context that surrounds and envelops the garden. Over the years, the arboretum has also become a practice-ground for landscape architects in the region, and today boasts more designs by more designers than possibly any other garden around.

Few have had the impact on the contemporary gardens of Wisconsin that Dennis Buettner has. Based in Fox Point, Buettner has focused his landscape practice on botanical garden design. He is responsible for the revival of several older gardens—including the Boerner Botanical Garden and the Janesville Rotary Gardens—and the creation of several new gardens—the Green Bay Botanical Garden, Allen Centennial Garden, and the restoration of Villa Terrace in Milwaukee. Buettner refers to his little corner of the world as the "pearl necklace," because of the significant garden spaces located in a relatively small area.

OPPOSITE: *Spring arrives at the Minnesota Landscape Arboretum in a blaze of color*

Afar from the fray is Glensheen, located on the shores of Lake Superior in the northern city of Duluth, Minnesota. Glensheen was built at the turn of the century, during the iron boom that brought great wealth to the area. The house and setting are remarkable, especially in the peak summer season when southern regions can seem burnt out. Here the cool lake breezes makes a stroll through the sloped, formal gardens pleasant at all times. Farther south, on the shores of Lake Minnetonka, outside of Minneapolis, the Noernberg estate dates to the same period. The old main house is long gone, but the gardens have been preserved as a talisman of the past, when large hotels and mansions dotted the shores of this summer retreat.

Perhaps the greatest pleasure a tour of gardens in the upper Midwest region reveals is the overwhelming interest in gardening from town to town. The public gardens and conservatories of Wisconsin are filled to capacity on weekends, especially during the winter when people come here looking for some sort of respite from the unyielding climate. During summer, places like the Rotary Gardens in Janesville, bubble with activity—whether from local gardeners working the soil or visitors watching in awe.

One of the many gardens at the Minnesota Landscape Arboretum

I

Milwaukee:
Boerner Botanical Gardens

LOCATION: OFF HIGHWAY 100 AND FOREST HOME AVENUE, TEN MILES SOUTH-
WEST OF DOWNTOWN

GARDEN OPEN: 8 am to sunset
daily, April–October; closed
November–March.
ADMISSION: free.

FURTHER INFORMATION FROM:
Milwaukee County Parks,
5879 92nd Street, Hales
Corners 53130
(414) 425-1130
www.uwm.edu/dept/biol-
ogy/boerner/index.htm

NEARBY SIGHTS OF INTEREST:
Milwaukee County Zoo, Saint
Josephat's Basilica

Landscape architect Alfred Boerner, who came of age in the
1920s, was thoroughly schooled in the Beaux-Arts style. This is
evident in the gardens he designed, which today bear his name,
and his well-known and unwavering philosophy: landscape
should be as much about education and respite as it should be
about beauty. Boerner was landscape architect for Milwaukee
County when Charles Witnall, an influential bureaucrat, real-
ized his dream for a large regional park on the outskirts of
town. As part of his work on the Witnall Park, Boerner
designed and built a botanical garden. The garden core is wonderfully geometric with major and minor axes culminating in
formal planting areas and a fountain as the focal point.

The *Annual Garden*, enclosed within a wall, lies at the
entrance to the site. Originally large elm trees anchored the
wildly colorful space, but today only one remains. In the center
of the space sits a fountain and a Pfitzer juniper next to it,
planted when the gardens opened in the 1940s. The statues
that adorn this space, and many that are found elsewhere in the
garden at large, were produced during the depression as part of
a WPA project. From here the gardens open up in to consecu-
tive grass-lined walks with various gardens laid out along them.
Preeminent among these is the *Daylily Walk*, which features
thousands of hemerocallis that bloom vibrantly in the summer.
Another treat is the *Rock Garden*, an intimate woodland space
containing wildflowers and several small streams. The garden
was also constructed during the Depression in the 1930s, and
the abundance of enthusiastic workers were able to bring in
more than 1,000 tons of limestone from local sources, which
Boerner arranged to give the space depth. Adjacent to this
space is the *Shrub Mall*. This is essentially a border garden
modeled on those developed by the English gardeners William
Robinson and Gertrude Jekyll. The long mall narrows at its
south end to give the illusion that it is longer than it really is.
The plant materials include irises and peonies as well as several
ornamental trees, such as the Amur chokeberry.

A garden house located on the grounds hosts a set of
revolving displays that continue in the winter when the outdoor
exhibits are closed. The park itself is a notable landscape, with
an incredible collection of old trees that are a testament to
Boerner's sensibilities and Witnall's pluck. A high point occurs
around Mother's Day when thousands of crabapples burst
into bloom.

GARDEN OPEN: 9 am to 5 pm daily. **ADMISSION:** $4.00 adults, $2.50 persons with disabilities and children 6–17 years.

FURTHER INFORMATION FROM: 524 Layton Boulevard, Milwaukee 53215 (414) 649-9830

NEARBY SIGHTS OF INTEREST: Haggerty Museum of Art, Pabst Mansion

2 Milwaukee: Mitchell Park Conservatory

LOCATION: PIERCE STREET AND LAYTON BOULEVARD IN MITCHELL PARK, WEST SIDE OF CITY

The three domes that comprise this conservatory are actually conoidal (bee-hive shaped) rather than spherical like more common geodesic structures. Designed by local architect Donald Grieb in 1959, the hope was that this unusual approach would better control the heat. Within this context, the design has been a success, in that the collections here are healthy, but also because the high arching architecture provides a wonderfully airy and light setting for landscape. Two domes house permanent collections of tropical and arid plants, respectively. Five desert regions are represented in the *Arid Dome*: Southwest America, Africa, Madagascar, South America, and Mexico. An "oasis" in the center of the structure serves as a gathering place for others that don't fit into these categories. Palms provide a high arching canopy, underplanted by cacti and succulents—all the while wild birds swoop through the air to great effect. "A world away from Wisconsin" is the theme of the *Tropical Dome*. Mahogany, chocolate, banana, and orchids are just a few of the over 450 different species that bulge this 15,000-square-foot space. The last dome is devoted to specialty shows. Five seasonal shows (such as poinsettias at Christmas) demarcate the year, while eclectic theme displays, such as a Charles Dickens' London and a Japanese Garden, are exhibited during interim periods. Outside the domes is the historic *Sunken Garden,* designed in a strict Victorian manner, with bedded annuals laid out in a wide rectangle of grass. These date back to the original conservatory in 1904.

GARDEN OPEN: 10 am to 6 pm daily, May–October. Call for off-season hours. **ADMISSION:** $3 adults, $1 children 5–12 years.

FURTHER INFORMATION FROM: 2600 Larsen Road, Green Bay 54303 (414) 490-9457

NEARBY SIGHTS OF INTEREST: Green Bay Packers

3 Green Bay: Green Bay Botanical Garden

LOCATION: EXIT 168 OFF HIGHWAY 41, AT THE INTERSECTION OF PACKERLAND AND LARSON ROADS

Like children, young gardens can be either boisterous and unruly, or shy and reserved. At times the Green Bay Botanical Garden is both of these. The garden, which opened in 1996, is in its first phase of development. The overall plan and design of many of the first gardens was executed by Dennis Buettner, an experienced botanical garden designer who has worked on many in the area. As an outdoor facility, the garden focuses on hardy plants that flourish in Green Bay's harsh climate. The first garden that visitors encounter is an ever-changing four seasons display, which in Wisconsin means it has been designed to retain interest during the winter with the inclusion of berried plants and interesting branching habits. Buettner has placed this garden in the entry, in the middle of a circular drive, to give the sense of enclosure (or immersion) in a unique space. For seasoned garden travelers the rest of garden may seem bare pickings, but it must be remembered that unlike its sister disciplines of art, sculpture, and architecture, landscape design always relies on the cooperation of mother nature—a collaborator that marches to her own drummer.

Other gardens that will exist in 2000 include an oval garden of perennials, a cottage garden that reproduces this English style based on the writings of William Robinson and Gertrude Jekyll, and a children's garden complete with maze, pond, and insect house, among other attractions. Part of an old orchard was conserved during construction and forms the backbone to an unusual orchard garden, featuring a display of naturalized spring bulbs stitched into the ground plane beneath the crooked trunks of apple trees. The garden has plans to add a rose garden, a small prairie, and several other theme and idea gardens as part of its public education mission. Like all things in the public realm, the timing of these is intimately entwined with funding processes. But judging from the enthusiasm and commitment of the present staff, it seems obvious that Green Bay is on the path to enjoying one of the better botanical gardens around.

With a good plan and design, newcomer Green Bay Botanical Garden promises to quickly join Wisconsin's "pearl necklace."

4 Oshkosh: Paine Art Center

LOCATION: NORTH OF TOWN AND THE UNIVERSITY OF WISCONSIN, OSHKOSH CAMPUS; CORNER OF CONGRESS STREET AND ROUTE 41

GARDEN OPEN: 11 am to 4 pm Monday–Sunday.
ADMISSION: free.
ART CENTER OPEN: 11 am to 4 pm Monday–Sunday. Admission: $5.00 adults, $2.50 seniors, free children under 12 years.

FURTHER INFORMATION FROM: 1410 Algoma Boulevard, Oshkosh 54901 (920) 235-6903

NEARBY SIGHTS OF INTEREST: Oshkosh Public Art Museum, Bergstrom-Mahler Museum

When lumber magnate Nathan Paine built this summer house in 1929 he wanted to surround it with symbols of his wealth. Instead of self-adulatory artwork or the pretentious English landscape garden, Paine opted for a timber forest that looks more at home in the Pacific northwest than in Wisconsin. Stitched into the woodlands are informal and formal gardens. Chief among the former is the *Primrose Path,* a romantic nature walk through delicate English primrose, which is a delight in the spring. Also found on the grounds is the *Sunken Garden,* which is hidden within a seemingly ancient wall and surrounded by a hedge. The design was inspired by Hampton Court in England, and the plant material includes both perennial and annuals, set around a central fountain. The 3.3-acre woodland includes diverse trees, including native species that have grown quite large over seventy years. Beneath the ample windows of the breakfast room is a white garden, situated around a loggia and enclosed by boxwood. One side is symmetrically designed in a crisscross pattern of

impatiens, while the other is composed as drifts of differently textured white-blooming plants, including Solomon seal and many spring bulbs. Set on the terrace, the white theme is carried out in various pots. There is also a radial herb garden, quartered by four walking paths leading to a sundial. The beds are designed in mixed layers, according to leaf texture rather than taxon or use.

The residence now houses an art collection, which extends into the landscape in the form of several sculptural pieces set about. The main attraction remains as Paine first envisioned: the magnificent woodlands that engulf the site.

5 Madison: Allen Centennial Garden

LOCATION: CORNER OF BABCOCK AND OBSERVATORY DRIVES, ON THE CAMPUS OF THE UNIVERSITY OF WISCONSIN

GARDEN OPEN: Dawn to dusk daily. **ADMISSION:** free.

FURTHER INFORMATION FROM: Facilities Management, (608) 262-1234

NEARBY SIGHTS OF INTEREST: University art gallery, State Historical Museum

Teaching gardens are usually bland. With raised "test beds" and rows of experimental hybrids, these gardens are typically oriented toward the scientist more than the artist. This is not the case in the Allen Centennial Garden, a new teaching garden for the University of Wisconsin's horticulture department. Designed by alumnus and local landscape architect Dennis Buettner, the garden addresses both horticultural and design ideas. The designed areas include a Victorian garden, a collection of exotic shrubs, an English perennial garden, and an Italian garden. The tour feels a bit like school—a sampling of everything to some heterogeneous end—and the garden succeeds remarkably. Part of this is Buettner's sensitive understanding of how the two-acre site works. The gardens, which wind around a grand old Victorian house (now the residence of the dean), move into one another seamlessly. A small watercourse provides a spine that ties several of the spaces together. In the formal gardens, architectural adornment helps to define and focus the intent. For example, in the English garden we find a reproduction of a Chippendale bridge, a classic example of British chinoisserie. The horticultural gardens include traditional collections of exotics as well as natives that reflect the growing interest in the science of ecology. To this end, there is a Wisconsin wildflower garden, a recycling display, and a bog. The centerpiece for many visitors will be the wonderfully overplanted New American garden, which showcases the latest eclecticism in U. S. gardening. Derived in part from the English cottage style, the aesthetic here is large and bold strokes of plant

An abundance of color radiates around the Paine Art Center.

material. But the American garden employs a broader plant vocabulary (some might say overblown or grotesque), such as chard, ornamental grasses, and cabbages.

The gardens are relatively young, having been built-out fully in only the last couple of years. Because they play an integral role in campus life, they are well maintained and every year come closer to their full potential.

A teaching garden and thing of beauty—both apply to the Allen Centennial Garden.

6 Madison: Olbrich Botanical Gardens

LOCATION: CORNER OF FAIR OAKS AND ATWOOD AVENUES, ON THE EASTERN SHORE OF LAKE MONONA, ONE MILE SOUTH OF ROUTE 30

Many people are unaware of the great care and long planning that go into creating city parks. The parks of Boston, New York, and other cities large and small were conceived and built by civic-minded individuals who saw the need for open space in a growing urban environment. In the East, the era of city parks took place at the end of the nineteenth century; in the Midwest it occurred in the first years of the twentieth century, as economies matured and metropolises grew within the rural landscape.

Such was the case in Madison in the 1910s, when Michael Olbrich, an established attorney, began buying up land along the shore of Lake Monona. The railroad corridor that ran close by the lake at the time was filling up with industrial buildings, while houses arose on the other side. Olbrich acquired lot after lot with the intent of preserving the land for the city, until he finally owned over a half-mile of shoreline. He donated the land to the city, and Olbrich and the local parks department hired Ossian Cole (O. C.) Simonds, the Chicago landscape architect, to design an urban park. From the outset, Olbrich wanted a municipal flower garden as the park's centerpiece; when he died in 1929 the park was still struggling to get underway and flower planting was the farthest thing from most people's minds. In the 1950s, a group of citizens built a public greenhouse. Several were erected and added to until the 1980s when the city commissioned architect Stuart Gallagher to design a pyramidal conservatory. A single, airy room contains a selection of tropical rainforest plants. The design weaves together specimens from various genus into a pastiche of color, texture, and smell. A circuitous pathway ramps up and down around its course to alter and vary the viewing experience, at once

GARDEN OPEN: 9 am to 5 pm daily, September–May; 9 am to 8 pm, June–August.
ADMISSION: free.
CONSERVATORY OPEN: 10 am to 4 pm Monday–Saturday; 10 am to 5 pm Sunday.
ADMISSION: $1 adults, free children under 5 years; free, 10 am to noon Wednesday and Saturday.

FURTHER INFORMATION FROM:
3330 Atwood Avenue, Madison 53704
(608) 246-4550
www.olbrich.org

NEARBY SIGHTS OF INTEREST:
Madison Museum of Art

A perennial garden lies beyond the exterior of the Bolz Conservatory at the Olbrich Botanical Gardens.

bringing us above the displays, and then carrying us below to feel immersed in the luxuriant foliage. Hundreds of butterflies and free-flying tropical birds swirling through the air lend an animated spirit to the garden.

Outside the conservatory, the landscape has been designed in a series of formal flower gardens, fulfilling the original dream of Olbrich. The *Great Lawn,* an ellipse defined along its southwest edge by a semicircular arbor, acts as the centrifugal force around which all else revolves. There is a regionally renowned *Rose Garden,* designed along a radial scheme and containing some 650 plants, as well as a rare mid-western rock garden. Two recent features are an overlarge perennial walk along winding paths and a stream lined with local limestone. In late spring the mixed borders are vibrant, while annuals, contrasted against a young background of shrubs and trees, dominate July and August. The *Sunken Garden,* which follows a French structure of limestone terraces, perennial borders, and an elegant 80-foot long reflecting pool, is being restored at this writing.

Outside the formal garden areas is an urban forest that contains an excellent mix of Midwest natives and exotics from elsewhere. The wildflower meadow explodes in vibrant colors in spring.

GARDEN OPEN: dawn to dusk daily, year-round. **ADMISSION:** free.

FURTHER INFORMATION FROM:
1455 Palmer Drive,
Janesville 53545
(608) 752-3885
jvlnet.com/~gardens

NEARBY SIGHTS OF INTEREST:
Wisconsin Dells, Lincoln-Tallman House, University of Wisconsin

7 ## Janesville: Rotary Gardens

LOCATION: HIGHWAY 11, EXIT 175A OFF INTERSTATE 90

Although it may sound like a lofty premise for a garden of plants, the purpose of the Janesville Rotary Garden is to promote international understanding and peace. It does this by presenting garden traditions from around the world. Except for the absence of much third world material, the gardens, now in their tenth year, offer exquisite examples of European and New World styles. The centerpiece is the formal French garden, a *parterre* garden of low-lying hedge, featuring an aquatics-filled pond. Overlooking this area is a semicircular pergola covered with clematis and a small garden of roses, all arranged in a delicate manner reminiscent of Gallic traditions. Two English style gardens illustrate the varied history of Anglo gardens. One is a *sunken garden,* designed as a central lawn lined with borders of perennials. The other is an *English cottage garden,* an early-twentieth-century style in which the irregular floral combinations are in perfect counterpoint to the geometric formality of earlier gardens (which the sunken garden mimics). It features broad bands of color in impressionistic patterns set within rectangular beds. Filling out the Euro collage are Dutch (bulbs), Irish (greens), and Italian (statuary) gardens. Both the Chinese and

Japanese traditions are represented. The former is oriented upon a small pond and includes a parasol pavilion as its architectural frame and an effusion of plants—daylilies, forsythia, and gingko trees. The *Japanese garden* presents many garden themes: moss garden, dry stream, and azaleas.

One highlight of the gardens is observing the connections and disconnections between different European and Asian traditions and those that have evolved in North America in later times. To this end, the Rotary Garden includes an extensive North American room with ornamental grasses and perennials in a kind of suburban pastiche. There is also an arrangement of annuals meant to imitate the work of Brazilian landscape designer Roberto Burle Marx. The focus on native plants and on ecology, which has dominated American gardening over the past decade, is given ample expression here. A small prairie of grasses and forbs stands sentry at the corner of Palmer and Sharon Roads. On the far edge of a pond, creating a visual backdrop to the entire garden, is an array of Wisconsin wildflowers. Taken together the gardens are eclectic as the world.

Art, such as this work entitled Dialogue, *graces the grounds of the Janesville Rotary Gardens.*

CONSERVATORY OPEN: 10 am to 4 pm daily, October–March; 10 am to 6 pm daily, April–September.

JAPANESE GARDEN OPEN: 11 am to 6 pm Wednesday–Monday; 11 am to 8 pm Tuesday, Mother's Day (May)–Labor Day (September).

ADMISSION: $1.00 adults, $0.50 seniors and youth, free children under 6 years.

FURTHER INFORMATION FROM: 1325 Aida Place, Saint Paul 55103 (612) 487-8200

NEARBY SIGHTS OF INTEREST: Como Park, Como Zoo, World Theater, Walker Art Center, Guthrie Theater

The Como Conservatory has been a beacon during the cold Minnesota winters.

8 Saint Paul: Como Park Conservatory

LOCATION: AIDA PLACE, OFF LEXINGTON AVENUE, THREE MILES NORTHWEST OF DOWNTOWN

Horace W. Cleveland planned the Twin Cities park system in the 1880s, during a nationwide trend in the development of natural refuges for growing urban populations. Among the notable features Cleveland imparted to Como Park was (initially) a little-noticed German horticulturist, Frederick Nussbaumer. Nussbaumer had worked at the Royal Botanical Gardens in England and an major nursery in France by the time Cleveland met him (reportedly) in Paris. As the story is told, the elder Cleveland was taken with the young Nussbaumer's knowledge and, by various methods of persuasion, he convinced the energetic plantsman to return with him to the American Midwest to work in a newly constructed city park on the shores of Lake Como in Saint Paul. Nussbaumer rose through the ranks of city bureaucracy to become the superintendent of parks. Along the way he hatched an ambitious plan to construct a conservatory within the park. Many other cities at the turn of the century had already made their mark with impressive Victorian glasshouses—New York and Buffalo preeminent among them—and it must have seemed natural for Saint Paul, a rapidly growing metropolis, to want to follow. But Nussbaumer had more sincere motives. He was a horticulturist, and like the intrepid plant explorers of his age he desired to create a place to cultivate plants for summer displays in the park

Ever since it was constructed in 1912 the Como Conservatory has fulfilled these two missions, to provide the citizens of the city with a gentile display of nature's opulence and to serve as the greenhouse for Como Park. As Nussbaumer

conceived it, these two ideas never diverged; one flowed easily into the other. The entrance hall of the conservatory is dedicated to mature palms, which have grown up in a series of concentric beds to reach for the pinnacle of the 64-foot dome. Along the groundplane are succulent displays of bromeliads and orchids. Notice the different types of agave, or "century plant," scattered about the display. The conservatory's devotion to this plant stems from the exciting occurrence in 1963 of a single specimen blooming at the rate of a dramatic nine inches per day. The stalk pressed against the roof within weeks, and the garden staff removed the glass and allowed it to peak. The event attracted media attention and a contest was undertaken to guess the number of blooms, for which a "century note" ($100) was given. A young boy of thirteen took the prize with his guess of 732 blooms. Ever since, this strange and frustratingly slow plant has had a permanent home in the collections.

The north and south wings of the conservatory are devoted to functional and aesthetic endeavors, respectively. The north wing features a well-labeled display of tropical plants that are used in everyday life. The *sunken garden,* located in the south wing, is the conservatory's showcase, where opulent arrangements are rotated according to the season: winter sees Cyclamen and winter bulbs; spring and summer pass through the cycle of perennials. The designs are conceived and planted by both staff and outside designers, giving rise to a steady stream of original ideas—sometimes exciting, sometimes disappointing, always worth investigating.

In 1962 a torrential hail storm shattered more than half the conservatory's glass panes. The staff attempted a retrofit using translucent fiberglass, but over time these became opaque, threatening the plants. In 1983 the conservatory hired Winsor Faricy Architects to complete a multi-million-dollar restoration. The results, a decade in the making, have been well worth it. While so many other cities have seen their great glasshouses lost to the ravages of time, Saint Paul has made it conservatory a legacy for the future.

Outside the conservatory lies the *Japanese garden,* designed by Nagasaki landscape architect Masami Matsuda as a gift from the people of that city to the people of Saint Paul. The design style, called Sansui, is a type of viewing garden that attempts to mimic the interplay of mountains and water—an integral feature of *feng shui.* The experience is oriented around a central water feature and a large "viewing stone" observable from the magnificently detailed tea house. Several stone lanterns, remnants of the St. Louis World's Fair of 1904, dot the landscape.

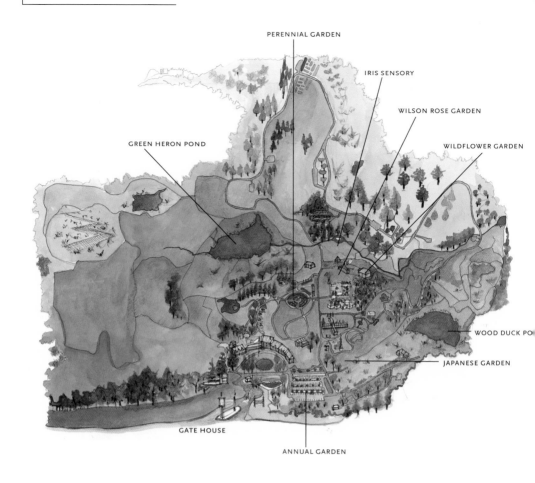

PERENNIAL GARDEN

IRIS SENSORY

WILSON ROSE GARDEN

WILDFLOWER GARDEN

GREEN HERON POND

WOOD DUCK PO

JAPANESE GARDEN

GATE HOUSE

ANNUAL GARDEN

9 Chanhassen: Minnesota Landscape Arboretum

LOCATION: HIGHWAY 5, TWENTY MILES SOUTHWEST OF MINNEAPOLIS

GARDEN OPEN: 8:00 am to sunset daily, May–September; 8:00 am to 5:30 pm daily, November–April. ADMISSION: $5 adults; free children; group discounts.

FURTHER INFORMATION FROM: 3675 Arboretum Drive, Chanhassen 55317 (612) 443-2460 www.arboretum.umn.edu

NEARBY SIGHTS OF INTEREST: Canterbury Downs, Renaissance Festival

The well-worn image of garden clubs—elderly ladies wearing flowered hats and "fiddling" in the garden—has nothing to do with the Minnesota Landscape Arboretum. This 935-acre naturalistic garden was conceived and originated by the Men's Garden Club of Minneapolis. In 1958 Archie Flack, an onion and potato broker who had been educated in horticulture at Kew Gardens in England, along with a few comrades in plantsmanship persuaded the University of Minnesota to sponsor a public garden along the border of its plant breeding facility south of the Twin Cities. Although a fledgling enterprise at first, the landscape arboretum managed to secure the Kansas City landscape architecture firm Hare and Hare to prepare a master plan. This original plan envisioned formal gardens close in a central structure, with an expanse of landscape gardens spreading out over the site.

As the name suggests, much of the garden's vast acreage is given over to naturalistic landscapes. Artfully managed by arboretum staff, the grounds include woodland and prairie types, with various tree and shrub collections woven into the hilly topography. In the springtime and early summer the *Azalea Research Trail*, two rows of mixed azaleas, burn to life, giving the green landscape sharp contrast. There is also a *hedge garden,* in which different types of evergreen and deciduous hedge varieties are displayed in windbreak fashion. The landscape gardens are accessible on foot or by tram-tour, which circuits the three-mile road system.

A series of formally designed gardens are located around the visitor center. Providing an appropriate buffer between wild and artifice is the *Woodland Azalea Garden,* a meticulously layered forest of mature canopy trees and informally arranged shrub azaleas, centered upon a kidney-shaped pool lined by tufa. Many of these varieties were cultivated at the arboretum and are tailored to the harsh climate. Mixing it up a bit are large leafed *petasites* and *amelancher.* The ground layer is underplanted with a rich array of wildflowers and ferns that give way, as we descend down the path, to the *Hosta Glade* of naturalized hostas. Closer to the center of the arboretum the gardens become even more elaborate. The *Sensui Tei Garden* was designed by Japanese garden designer Koichi Kawana. The garden applies a traditional Japanese form of the "garden pure water" to the Minnesota context, mixing the inner logic of the form with the local plant palette and climatological character. A waterfall provides the central image, and is planted about with expressive jack pines and weeping beech. Small and intimate,

OPPOSITE: *Broad expanses, expressive of the glacial terrain, describe the Minnesota Landscape Arboretum.*

the garden is organized around a central path with various viewing areas arranged from each side to contemplate the central scene. Nearby, the *Palma J. Wilson Rose Garden* is a must-see during the height of the summer, when a clique of seductive hybrids burst on the scene. An simple trellis, designed by Saint Paul architect Edwin Lundie, supports an dense display of clematis.

Lundie also designed the Snyder building, an English country manor named after the arboretum's director for many years, Leon C. Snyder. Immediately behind the center is a new terrace garden, with a small water feature and beds of perennials. The pathway ascends from here through displays of lilies, peonies, daylilies, and lilacs. The climb ends in an oval of perennial beds, centered on a pool, and from which there are views downslope to a small cloistered garden and fragrance garden that seem hidden from the world at large.

At the far end of the formal garden areas lies the sensory garden, a delicately arranged garden enclosed by walls; raised beds elevate plant materials so that the disabled can enjoy them. Selections are chosen for olfactory and textural features to also appeal to blind visitors. The entrance to the garden, among the more beautiful places at the Arboretum, features a well-balanced allée of crabapples, set around a trimmed panel of grass. Perhaps it is the youthfulness of the design, or the plant combinations, or the geometric balance, but this space has an ineffable presence—and several benches are there to enjoy.

The arboretum has become a locus for landscape architects around the country to design garden spaces. Besides Hare and Hare, the roster includes John Simonds (son of O.C.), Michael Van Valkenburgh, Ellerbee Beckett, and Jim Hagstrom, who has recently designed the *Terrace Garden*.

OPPOSITE: *Sculpture and other public art enliven a wintry scene.*

BELOW: *Gazebo in the Palma J. Wilson Rose Garden*

IO # Wayzata: Noernberg Gardens

LOCATION: NORTH SHORE DRIVE, ON CRYSTAL BAY, LAKE MINNETONKA

GARDEN OPEN: 7:00 am to 8:00 pm weekdays, 8:00 am to 8:00 pm weekends, April–August; 8:00 am to 3:30 pm weekdays, 9:00 am to 5:00 pm weekends, September–October 15. **ADMISSION:** free.

FURTHER INFORMATION FROM: 2840 North Shore Drive, Wayzata 55391 (612) 475-0050

NEARBY SIGHTS OF INTEREST: Canterbury Downs, Valleyfair, Eloise Butler Wildflower Garden

A native plant palette and Asiatic architectural features comprise Noernberg Gardens.

In the 1890s Lake Minnetonka was Minneapolis's Newport—an affluent summer watering hole. This is where the swelling millionaire class, who was making its fortunes in everything from railroads to beer, built its hotels, casinos, and lavish mansions. Many of these, including James Hill's 800-room Lafayette Hotel, have since been ruined. None boasted a garden landscape more superb than brewery magnate Frederick Noernbeg, one of the original founders of Grain Belt Beer. Noernberg built a large Queen Anne mansion on the shore of Crystal Bay on the lake, which has since been demolished. A set of free-standing columns that mark the old foundation are all that is left, as well as the gardens that are tended by the parks department. The tree collection was drawn from species worldwide, however Noernberg accentuated his Germanic heritage with an emphasis on birch and evergreens. Throughout the landscape are many unusual rocks placed to creates structure and focal points. Most of these were collection by Noernberg's daughter Winnie, a horticulturist, who traveled the world. The daylily and azalea collections are two main attractions. The first encompasses a large area, and in early summer literally explodes in color. Because of the stringy stalks of the plants and the fact that they are green much of the time, the design of this garden favors tight bunching of the plant material. The *Azalea Garden* showcases a solid collection of Northern Lights, an azalea developed at the nearby Minnesota Landscape Arboretum specifically to tolerate the harsh climate here. These typically bloom in May. Within the garden you will also find a number of architectural remnants from the Noernberg estate, such as the boathouse redesigned with a pagoda-like roof by Frederick Noernberg after a trip to Japan. The fence surrounding the property is also original. In recent years the county parks managers have introduced native plantings, such as grasses and prairie wildflowers, which is in keeping with Noernberg and his daughter's own interest in the botany of Minnesota. To this end the landscape features a healthy selection of meadow rue, astilbe, Joe Pye weed, and lady's mantle—which dazzle from late spring and deep into fall.

11 Duluth: Glensheen and the Duluth Rose Garden

LOCATION: GLENSHEEN IS LOCATED ALONG ROUTE 61, NORTH OF THE CITY; DULUTH ROSE GARDEN IS IN LEIF ERICSON PARK

For the last half century Duluth has been a vacation spot for residents in the Twin Cities, who come here to enjoy the chilly waters of Lake Superior. At the turn of the century it was also an up-and-coming city, owing to the great wealth that came from the iron-rich ground to the north. While there were several millionaires in Duluth at that time, perhaps none made their mark as strongly as Chester Adgate Congdon, a transplant from New York City who served in various executive roles with area businesses. Congdon built Glensheen, an English country manor designed by architect Clarence Johnston and furnished by the William French Company, both of Saint Paul. For the grounds, Congdon brought in an engineer, Charles Leavitt of New York. Before the facade, Leavitt created a parterre and fountain garden, with central lawn panel, brick paths, and an abundance of perennials and vines to soften the balustrades and architectural adornment. The fountain is French inspired with a rectangular base hosting a bare assortment of lilies. In the side garden, which lies on a gentle slope toward with the lake in the background, is a selection of annuals and perennials "bedded-out" in a geometric scheme around a sundial. The canvas, a well-tended lawn, gives the highly rigid design a tinge of informality. Downslope from here is an abundant vegetable garden that has been cultivated with period plants by the University of Minnesota, which has used the garden as a research plot for many years.

The Leif Ericson Park in downtown Duluth also features a lovely rose garden that is meticulously cared for. It is at its peak throughout June, long after other rose gardens die away, owing to the northerly latitudes. There are over 3,000 plants in the collection, neatly arranged around a gazebo on the lake.

GARDEN OPEN: 9:30 am to 4:00 pm daily, May–October; 11:00 am to 2:00 pm Sundays, November and December; 11:00 am to 2:00 pm Friday–Sunday, January–March; 11:00 am to 2:00 pm daily, April.
ADMISSION TO GARDENS: free.
ADMISSION TO HOUSE: $8.75 adults, $7.00 seniors and children 12–15 years, $4.00 children 6–11 years.

FURTHER INFORMATION FROM:
3300 London Road,
Duluth 55804
(888) 454-GLEN
www.d.umn.edu/glen

NEARBY SIGHTS OF INTEREST:
Tweed Museum of Art,
Karpeles Manuscript
Museum

Gleensheen offers a study in formal sophistication on the shores of Lake Superior.

IOWA

5

DUBUQUE

3

2

4

1

CEDAR RAPIDS

DES MOINES

COUNCIL BLUFFS

6

7

QUAD CITIES

11

KANSAS CITY

12

COLUMBIA

8

9

ST. LOUIS

10

MISSOURI

SPRINGFIELD

1 Des Moines: Des Moines Botanical Center
2 Madrid: Iowa Arboretum
3 Ames: Reiman Gardens
4 Cedar Rapids: Brucemore
5 Dubuque: Dubuque Arboretum and Botanical Garden
6 Clinton: Bickelhaupt Arboretum
7 Davenport: VanderVeer

8 Saint Louis: The Jewel Box
9 Saint Louis: Missouri Botanical Garden
10 Gray Summit: Shaw Arboretum
11 Centralia: Chance Gardens
12 Kingsville: Powell Gardens

MISSISSIPPI VALLEY REGION:

Iowa and Missouri

A concentration of gardening is to be found in the center of Iowa, a triangular area defined by Des Moines, Madrid, and Ames. Much of the energy emanates from Des Moines, one corner of this trinity. Not only is the influential Des Moines Botanical Center located here, but also several gardening magazines make their home in this Midwestern town, and often it can be hard to find someone without a hard set of ideas about gardens and gardening. The Botanical Center has become a magnate for gardening activities, in part because it invites garden designers from afar to add frequently to the *River Walk* of gardens. The second point of the triangle is formed by the quiet town of Madrid, with the passive Iowa Arboretum. The university town of Ames completes the figure, home of the fast-growing Reiman gardens, a public demonstration garden.

More than anything, Iowa is home to arboreta and botanical gardens. The Bickelhaupt Arboretum is a beautiful, old garden that takes advantage of its natural setting to display a quirky collection of plants. The Dubuque Arboretum and Botanical Garden is much newer—although most of the collections are well filled out. In the coming years we can add yet another of these public educational institutions to the list: the Cedar Valley Arboretum and Botanical Garden in Waterloo, Iowa, which at this printing was just getting underway. Amid all these botanical gardens, Brucemore stands out as the only estate garden in Iowa, and it's English style gardens are well worth the visit.

OPPOSITE: *A hardy collection of crabapple trees at the Bickelhaupt Arboretum in Clinton*

From Saint Louis, the Missouri Botanical Garden has exerted a powerful influence over gardens in the region, in the Midwest at large, and across the country. In fact, one might even make the case that it is the most important garden in the United States. It is a major research institution and public garden that encourages several visits and this without revealing all its secrets. Also located within the Saint Louis is the Jewel Box. While the collections are fairly standard, the Art Deco architecture is stunning.

Potted displays at Chance Gardens in Centralia, Missouri

Missouri is a large state, and garden enthusiasts should consider venturing out to Kingsville to visit the Powell Gardens. Again, the architecture is a major lure, considering the garden boasts one of the most spectacular outdoor chapels designed by Fay Jones, who was awarded the American Institute of Architects Gold Medal in 1990.

Des Moines: Des Moines Botanical Center

LOCATION: EAST RIVER DRIVE, JUST OFF INTERSTATE 235, NEAR THE CAPITOL

Des Moines is a gardening center for Iowa and a large, interstate region. For starters, several gardening magazines are located here. Importantly, the Des Moines Botanical Center, the city's major public garden, is located on fourteen acres along the Des Moines River banks. The centerpiece of the garden is the striking geodesic dome, which rises eighty feet at its center. Surrounding the stately palms, the collections include a full range of glasshouse species, including an arid zone, subtropical, and the full show of cycads, ferns, and vines. Of particular note is the Hirsch/Ladany Bonsai Collection, which includes several plants that are over a hundred years old. Many consider it one of the best in the country.

Outside the dome are acres of informal and formal gardens. The main feature is the River Walk, along which are placed successive perennial gardens. All are new since the flood of 1993 and show the hand of many different local designers. Several of the gardens are color-themed, including the *Blue Wave*, composed with sage, ornamental grasses, coreopsis, and plenty of dainty anemones, and the *White Garden*, designed in the English cottage garden style with large drifts of peonies, roses, and lilies that exudes an old-time flavor. Recent additions to the walk are the new *Butterfly Garden* and the intelligent *Hillside Garden* designed by locals Ann Hutchinson and Barbara Lyford. Only four plant species are used in this vertical tapestry: viburnum, miscanthus, sumac, and pennisetum. It is wondrously alive in autumn. Daylilies, asters, and a sizable garden of phlox are all significant features of the garden; however what attracts many studious gardeners is the herb garden, one of the largest herb collections for a thousand miles and lovingly administered by a local garden group. The plants are arranged by use, and include sections on industrial, dye, biblical, medicinal, and prairie herbs, among others. The entrance to the gardens is marked by the eye-catching *Rainbow* sculpture.

GARDEN OPEN: 10 am to 6 pm Monday–Thursday; 10 am to 9 pm Friday; 10 am to 5 pm Saturday and Sunday.
ADMISSION: $1.50 adults, $0.75 seniors, $0.50 children and students.

FURTHER INFORMATION FROM: 909 East River Drive, Des Moines 50316
(515) 242-2734

NEARBY SIGHTS OF INTEREST: Des Moines Arts Center, Zoo

Local designers have contributed to an evolving quilt of gardens at the Des Moines Botanical Center.

2 Madrid: Iowa Arboretum

GARDEN OPEN: Sunrise to sunset daily. **ADMISSION:** $2 adults, free children under 12 years.

FURTHER INFORMATION FROM:
1875 Peach Avenue,
Madrid 50156
(515) 795-3216

NEARBY SIGHTS OF INTEREST:
Wildlife exhibit and research station, Reiman Gardens

LOCATION: OFF STATE ROUTE E-57, TWO-AND-A-HALF MILES SOUTHWEST OF LUTHER, IN BOONE COUNTY

A "library of living plants" is a distinctly European idea, born in the late Victorian period when science—particularly the life sciences, impelled by Charles Darwin—was making rapid advances. Over the years, the American twist on this idea has evolved into something less haughty, if more patriotic. Gone are the intrepid plant explorers, arrived are the preservers of local flora who struggle heroically against the plow to retain a region's landscape. The Iowa Arboretum, like so many others, is one of these living libraries. Established in the 1960s, the arboretum (which is still considered somewhat young) contains a diverse selection of trees and naturalistic landscape native to Iowa. Within the three-hundred acre woodland are several garden areas, set next to streams or littered beneath the canopy in carpets of color. The emphasis is on identification, and each plant is appropriately labeled. At the entrance, near the arboretum center, are large demonstration gardens of irises, roses, herbs, and ornamental grasses. A central gazebo, set on a slight grassy knoll and surrounded by specimen trees provides a focal point for exploring the garden.

3 Ames: Reiman Gardens

GARDEN OPEN: Dawn to dusk daily, May–October.
ADMISSION: free.

FURTHER INFORMATION FROM:
Iowa State University,
Ames 50011
(515) 294-0028
www.ag.iastate.ed/agcoll/rei
mangardens.html

NEARBY SIGHTS OF INTEREST:
Wildlife Research Station

ABOVE: *Prairie flowers, such as this coneflower, are featured at the Iowa Arboretum.*

LOCATION: ELWOOD DRIVE, SOUTHWEST OF THE STADIUM AT IOWA STATE UNIVERSITY

Iowa State University is among the country's best schools of higher education for horticulture, so it should come as no surprise that the school also hosts an impressive garden. For years the horticulture gardens were located on a small three-quarter- acre site deep within the campus. In 1993 alumnus Roy Reiman donated the money to expand the gardens in a nine-acre site at the entrance of the school. The gardens were initially master -planned by CLR Design of Philadelphia; based on this blueprint, various local firms have individually designed each garden area. An educational center, named for the former head of the horticulture department, is the focal point of all activity in the gardens. Besides academic pursuits, the center hosts an array of public education events, including a significant master gardeners program. Although still in a build-out phase, several gardens have already been built and planted. Foremost among these is a rose garden containing many unusual rose hybrids developed here.

The most recent addition to the gardens is a home demonstration area where university staff offer regionally specific ideas for residential landscapes, such as how to use fences in a garden and what kinds of plants grow best in this climate. Beautiful, non-educational displays are also a part of the garden. One of the first areas to be designed was the *Campanile Garden,* located at the base of a contemporary architectural monument. Large swaths of annuals in bands of rainbow colors greet visitors as they arrive. There is also an herb garden arranged as an Elizabethan knot garden. The garden continues to receive new donations and is well along to its goal of 14 different garden areas. Although young, because of its association with the university the garden is wonderfully maintained.

4   Cedar Rapids: Brucemore

LOCATION: FOLLOW SIGNS FROM EXIT 22 OFF INTERSTATE 380, DOWNTOWN

Thomas Sinclair, Midwestern meat-packing magnate, and his wife Caroline, built Brucemore in 1886 as their countrified intown estate. George Douglas of the Quaker Oats Company purchased the original Queen Anne mansion in 1906 and extensively remodeled it. He hired Chicago landscape architect Ossian Cole (O. C.) Simonds to produce a master plan for the grounds. Simonds was an ardent advocate of planting with native midwestern plants, in the idiom of the prairie style; yet he was more flexible in his design ideas than contemporary landscape architect Jens Jensen, allowing his clients' tastes to prevail. Simonds' use of three-dimensional rooms carved out of wooded areas presents the strongest design theme in Brucemore's landscape, with a carpet of gentle lawn forming the vertical groundplane and the blue sky (ideally) overhead.

The gardens are the product of Mrs. Irene Hazeltine Douglas, George Douglas's wife, who devoted herself to cultivating the grounds as well as studying the art of garden design. She read the periodicals of the day, which no doubt brought her into contact with English garden designer and writer Gertrude Jekyll. This is apparent in the design of the perennial, or formal, garden located off the northeast side of the house. The beds are meticulously carved into the landscape in strict geometrical forms, while the planting patterns are naturalistic "drifts" of color that flow into one another. Closest to the house are rectangular beds lined in rows with arborvitae punctuation at each corner; at the far end, enclosed by a fence of climbing roses, are a pair of distinctive horseshoe-shaped arrangements that catch the eye from afar.

GARDEN OPEN: 10 am to 3 pm Tuesday–Saturday, February–December, by tour only. ADMISSION: $5 adults, $2 students 6–18 years.

FURTHER INFORMATION FROM: 2160 Linden Drive SE, Cedar Rapids 52403 (319) 362-7375 www.brucemore.org

NEARBY SIGHTS OF INTEREST: Granger House, Cedar Rapids Museum of Art

ABOVE: *Iowa State University's public gardens include both formal areas and naturalistic spaces.*

BELOW: *The Brucemore estate is enclosed by sumptuous gardens.*

Mrs. Douglas's tastes tended toward what we today might be termed "old fashioned" but which aligned with the cottage garden style of Jekyll, and included coreopsis, sweet William, and sweet peas. Today the garden presents a more contemporary look, with hostas and such accents as campanula and rudbeckia. In 1937 the Douglas's daughter Margaret and her husband Howard Hall moved to Brucemore and began training the landscape toward a more modern aesthetic.

Today Brucemore is owned and operated by the National Trust for Historic Preservation, which administers a thorough garden tour for visitors.

GARDEN OPEN: 8 am to sunset daily, Arbor Day–October; 9 am to 5 pm weekdays, 9 am to 1 pm Saturday, November–April.
ADMISSION: free.

FURTHER INFORMATION FROM:
3800 Arboretum Drive,
Dubuque 52001
(319) 556-2100

NEARBY SIGHTS OF INTEREST:
Highway 61, Crystal Lake Cave

Prairie flowers are in full bloom at the Dubuque Arboretum.

5 Dubuque: Dubuque Arboretum and Botanical Garden

LOCATION: IN MARSHALL PARK, WEST 32ND STREET, ON THE NORTHWEST SIDE OF THE CITY

The Dubuque Arboretum and Botanical Garden was founded in 1980 in Marshall Park, on 55 acres. The arboretum comprises much of the garden, and features both exotic ornamentals and native species. It also protects several woodland garden collections, including a nationally renowned hosta garden, designed in a curving manner and with a heterogeneous selection of plants—against a palette of stone retaining walls and shade trees. Several ponds and waterfall are located throughout the grounds to increase the visual and aural effect of the gardens. Located near the visitors center are several display gardens that are cultivated each summer and feature a good selection of lilies, dahlias, and, in the fall, chrysanthemums. The arboretum also features a formal herb garden of knots and geometric patterns, and one of the best rose gardens in the state of Iowa, organized in abundant, drifting borders around a bucolic trellised structure. Naturalists will enjoy the wildflowers and prairie grasses stitched into the arboretum, which change over the year from vibrant and spectacular in the spring to golden and mature in the fall. At the height of the summer season, the arboretum host a jazz group on most weekend evenings, performing in the open air amphitheater, the sound animating the gardens.

6 Clinton: Bickelhaupt Arboretum

LOCATION: CORNER OF SOUTH 14TH STREET AND FLORENCE AVENUE,
DOWNTOWN CLINTON, TWO MILES NORTH OF THE QUAD CITIES

GARDEN OPEN: Dawn to dusk
daily. **ADMISSION:** free.

FURTHER INFORMATION FROM:
340 South 14th Street, Clinton
52732-5432
(319) 242-4771

NEARBY SIGHTS OF INTEREST:
Showboat Museum,
Mississippi River

Alexis de Tocqueville once wrote that the Mississippi River divided the continent like a big scar. Actually, when you visit the mighty Mississippi what you find is that it gathers, rather than splits, pulling everything within a wide swath of territory toward its gently rolling waters. This becomes clear at the Bickelhaupt Arboretum, which is defined by the meandering Rock Creek. This diminutive watercourse cuts a path through the flat property before descending into the Mississippi only a mile away. Here, however, it forms the centerpiece to an intimate arboreta of ornamental trees and garden collections. Nestled in the small oxbows of the creek are several riparian gardens of grasses and flowers that cling to the sculpted banks as if magnetized. At one curved rise sits a well-tended prairie garden that extends up onto the flat top above the creek. A hardy collection of flowering viburnum and crabapple sits in the distance, accentuating the graceful dip of the land. The prize at the arboretum goes to the *lilacs,* which explode in color in the spring. They have received several national awards. Also featured are: an informal *rose garden;* a display of plants used in medicine; and an expanse of *dwarf conifers,* laid out in amoebae-like beds and set against a green canvas of lawn. An arrangement of columnar trees provide an architectural background. Although the plant selections are divided by taxon and planted in what could be called arrangements rather than conscious designs, the arboretum is an educational facility—including a library and museum on the grounds. Below this most practical of veneers is a magical landscape.

Unusual conifers are designed as individual pieces in the overall tapestry at Biklehaupt.

7 Davenport: VanderVeer

GARDEN OPEN: Dawn to dusk daily.

CONSERVATORY OPEN: 10 am to 4 pm Tuesday–Sunday.

ADMISSION: $0.50 Wednesday–Sunday; free Tuesdays; no fee in summer.

FURTHER INFORMATION FROM: 214 West Central Park Avenue, Davenport 52803 (319) 326-7818

NEARBY SIGHTS OF INTEREST: Putnam Museum, Museum of Art

A Burle Marx-esque aesthetic informs the original design of VanderVeer conservatory.

LOCATION: BETWEEN CENTRAL PARK AND LOMBARD STREET, HIGHWAY 61 OFF INTERSTATE 80

Like many conservatories, VanderVeer was once something much greater: a Victorian glasshouse designed and built by Lord and Burnham. The 1950s replacement was also constructed by this venerable firm, yet this structure is nondescript. Inside, however, overseen by landscape architect Susan Anderson, the main attraction is a series of hortifloral shows. These evolve throughout the year and present changing growing seasons. A permanent collection of palms and other tropicals reside on site, but most visitors gravitate to the effusion of azaleas in early spring . . . the cineraries and oriental lilies around Easter . . . the mums in the fall . . . the poinsettias around Christmas.

Outside of the conservatory, Anderson has cultivated several outdoor gardens. The centerpiece is an all-America display rose garden arranged in a formal radial design, with a pergola and fountain. There are several flower gardens, which are centered around a lagoon, a precious legacy from the original 1895 park design.

8 Saint Louis: The Jewel Box

LOCATED: CORNER OF WELLS AND MCKINLEY DRIVES IN FOREST PARK, WEST
SIDE OF THE CITY

When Forest Park was first laid out in 1874 it was a verdant pasture and woodlands—a good carriage ride from downtown to which city dwellers could retreat on a Saturday afternoon. After a hundred years the city has grown to encompass this 1,293-acre landscape, transforming it into a significant urban park. A major restoration is currently underway, including a "daylighting" of the old River des Peres that once ran through the area but is now contained in underground pipes. In the middle of the park, near the Zoo, lies the Jewel Box, a Depression-era conservatory—as eclectic as any garden in the country. The most striking feature is the architecture, conceived and designed by local engineer William C. E. Becker, in the 1930s. The Jewel Box is built like a "rectangular layer cake," quips one gardener and rises like an art deco diamond from its perch in the park. The glass walls are cantilevered and vault to almost fifty feet. The original purpose of the conservatory, according to local historians, was to preserve common yard plants in the 1920s that were dying in the face a proliferation of coal-burning residences polluted Saint Louis. Today the conservatory houses more typical fare, such as a permanent collection of tropicals. These are trimmed regularly as the structure depends for natural light from the airy glass walls. The center of the garden plays host to an ever-revolving seasonal flower display: lilies at Easter, hydrangeas for Mother's Day, azaleas in the late spring, bromeliads (hearts of flame) in the summer, mums for fall, and poinsettias at Christmas—and then all over again. Outside of the conservatory are summer gardens, winding tightly around the box, of classical sculptures and an evolving collection of flowers.

GARDEN OPEN: 9 am to 5 pm
daily. ADMISSION: $0.50.

FURTHER INFORMATION FROM:
St. Louis Parks Department,
(314) 531-1503
www.slfp.com/ForestParkJB.h
tm

NEARBY SIGHTS OF INTEREST:
St. Louis Art Museum,
Science Museum

An art deco conservatory provides a backdrop for St. Louis' public garden.

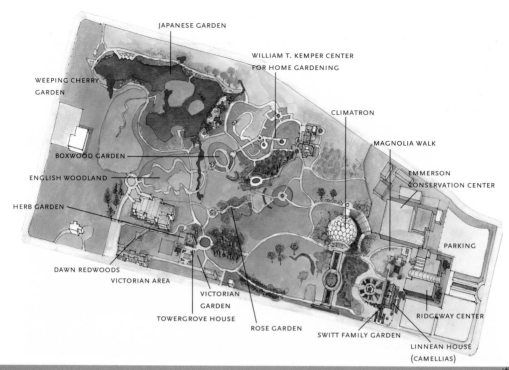

JAPANESE GARDEN

WILLIAM T. KEMPER CENTER
FOR HOME GARDENING

WEEPING CHERRY
GARDEN

CLIMATRON

MAGNOLIA WALK

BOXWOOD GARDEN

EMMERSON
CONSERVATION CENTER

ENGLISH WOODLAND

HERB GARDEN

PARKING

DAWN REDWOODS

VICTORIAN AREA

VICTORIAN
GARDEN

RIDGEWAY CENTER

TOWERGROVE HOUSE

ROSE GARDEN

SWITT FAMILY GARDEN

LINNEAN HOUSE
(CAMELLIAS)

9 Saint Louis: Missouri Botanical Garden

LOCATION: INTERSECTION OF VANDERVENTER PLACE AND SHAW BOULEVARD, FIVE MILES SOUTHWEST OF DOWNTOWN

GARDEN OPEN: 9 am to 8 pm daily, Memorial Day–Labor Day; 9 am to 5 pm daily, September–May; closed Christmas Day.

ADMISSION: $5.00 non resident visitors, $3.00 seniors and St. Louis residents, $1.50 St. Louis seniors, free children until 12 years and all on Wednesday and Saturday mornings.

FURTHER INFORMATION FROM: 4344 Shaw Boulevard, St. Louis 63110
(314) 577-9400
www.mobot.org

NEARBY SIGHTS OF INTEREST: Gateway Arch, Art Museum and Forest Park

OPPOSTIE: *The Linnean House (1882) is the oldest continually operating conservatory in the U.S.*

BELOW: *Pavilion and Tai Hu stone in the Margaret Grigg Nanjing Friendship Garden.*

Like so many good things in America, the Missouri Botanical Garden originated as an immigrant's dream. Englishman Henry Shaw landed on the western banks of the Mississippi at the sleepy metropolis of Saint Louis in 1819, and over the next twenty years made himself a fortune as the city grew up around him. One feature that most impressed Shaw about his adopted home (besides the economic opportunities it afforded) was the landscape—in particular the prairie lands of tall grasses that began to sprout just west of town, where the topography leveled out and the long march to the plains commenced. In 1839, after accumulating considerable wealth, Shaw purchased great tracts of the prairie. He built a fine palatial mansion, and then turned his attention to cultivating the landscape into a botanical garden. He was assisted in this endeavor, according to historians, by Dr. George Englemann, a German botanist and physicist, who persuaded Shaw to use as his model the European public gardens such as Royal Botanical Gardens at Kew, England. The duo sought the advice of the great Harvard botanist Asa Gray and Kew's director, Sir William Hooker. Over one-hundred years later, the Missouri Botanical Garden has evolved into one of the country's most significant research institutions, with an unparalleled library and a staff of experts. At the same time Shaw's original vision—to provide the public with a place to interact with and appreciate the natural environment—remains a central and primary focus.

One attraction is the geodesic dome, modeled on the drawings and writings of R. Buckminster Fuller, which houses the tropical collections. Scientifically dubbed the *Climatron*, the dome encloses a half-acre of rainforest. The collection is wildly fantastic, featuring among other alien plants, the famed double coconut that produces the largest seed in the plant kingdom. When the dome first opened in 1960 the panes were all Plexiglas, which clouded over in time; these were replaced with a treated glass in 1988, during a major renovation. Just north of the geodesic dome lies the *Shoenberg Temperate House,* constructed in 1990. Temperatures here are a little cooler and the plant palette focuses upon such Mediterranean themes as figs, olives, cork, and an assortment of riparian plants that thrive along riverbanks in semi-arid climates.

ABOVE: *Wheel-shaped Gladney Rose Garden*

BELOW: *The Moorish Garden in the Shoenberg Temperate House provides an example of Islamic garden design.*

In addition to the botanical selection, there is a *Moorish Garden* in the temperate house, designed according to the centuries-old garden traditions of Arabia and the Muslim world. The central feature of the Moorish garden is the wall, erected to protect the garden from desiccating winds and uncompromising sun. With the slightest water, a garden paradise would arise within this enclosure. This idea of paradise resonates through Muslim theology, and many Islamic mosques feature such gardens as integral to the architecture. Notice within this garden the vivid mosaics reminiscent of the great gardens of Isfahan and elsewhere in Islam.

A major feature of the garden is *Seiwa-En*, the Japanese garden. The name translates as "garden of pure, clear harmony and peace," and covers a total of fourteen acres, making it the largest Japanese garden in North America. The garden was designed in 1977 by Koichi Kawana, a professor of landscape architecture at the University of California, Los Angeles, and is derived from several different traditions. Much of the garden revolves around a massive central lake in the *kaiyu-shiki* or "wet strolling garden" style, popular in the nineteenth cen-

tury. A significant teahouse rests on an island in the middle of the lake. Closed to the public—partially as to indicate its sacredness in Japanese tradition—the teahouse is meant to serve as an architectural focus as you wander on the footpath around the lake and enjoy the different gardens. Among these are a dry garden of raked sand, boulders, and brilliant azaleas that break from the monochromatic presentation of much of the rest of the gardens. Throughout Seiwa-En the emphasis is on visual experience—carried along more by the depth of the artistic presentation than by any personal volition. In the spirit of Zen Buddhism, the monks of which were the primary caretakers of such gardens, Seiwa-En was consciously designed as a counterpoint to the frenetic pace of life. The best time in the garden is winter, when the snow accentuates the form of Kawana's peerless compositions.

ABOVE: *The Ridgeway Center visitors garden*

BELOW, TOP: *Mist over Seiwa-En, Japanese Garden, give visual definition to beds of raked sand*

BOTTOM: *Tower Grove House and mausoleum, former estate of Henry Shaw*

The Chinese garden contrasts with Seiwa-En. Designed in the "scholar's garden" style of Suzhou, the *Nanjing Friendship Garden*—so named after St. Louis's sister-city relationship with the Chinese city Nanjing—is a walled garden. The emphasis here is not upon plants and their arrangement against a visual canvas, as in Seiwa-En, but on the manipulation of volumetric space through architectural means. As you walk through the Chinese garden, the idea is to experience the space as it shifts. Changes in elevation, around small bodies of water, into and out of pagodas and small structures—the pathway through the garden twists and undulates in a rhythmic pattern that speaks less to the eyes than to the inner ear, or sense of equilibrium.

Education has become a natural outgrowth of the garden's research and public institution missions. The *William T. Kemper Center for Home Gardening* addresses itself to the needs of everyday gardeners, whether practical or fanciful. Arranged as a series of theme gardens, the center includes shade gardens, fragrance gardens, plant arrangements that attract butterflies and birds, and a secret garden. The *Center for Plant Conservation*, located near the entrance, is involved in pinpointing endangered species and initiating programs to save them. It administers a dry stream bed garden on-site.

Shaw's Victorian impulses can still be seen throughout the garden, in some places as remnant garden features, such as an allée of Osage orange trees, and in others as modern reinterpretations of the past. In 1994 an authentic Victorian garden was planted next

Seiwa-En is considered the most important Japanese garden in the U.S.

to the Shaw mansion, designed by Environmental Planning and Design of Pittsburgh. Bedded-out annuals provide eye-catching ground displays set within an architectural bower of hedge and walls. The mansion is open as a museum and features a display of period furniture and many of Shaw's belongings. A plethora of other gardens, designed on themes or donated by a coterie of philanthropists, fills out the collections. Interspersed throughout is an exquisite collection of sculpture that provides counterpoint and punctuation to this abundant landscape of botanica. The Missouri Botanical Garden is large in every sense of the word and garners the attention and examination than more than one visit can possibly afford.

GARDENS OPEN: 7 am to half-hour past sunset daily.
ADMISSION: $3 adults, $2 seniors, free children under 12 years.

FURTHER INFORMATION FROM:
P.O. Box 38,
Gray Summit 63039
(314) 451-3512
www.mobot.org/MOBOT/arb oretum

NEARBY SIGHTS OF INTEREST:
National Museum of Transportation

10 Gray Summit: Shaw Arboretum

LOCATION: HIGHWAY 100 AND PACIFIC STREET, TWENTY-TWO MILES SOUTH-WEST OF THE JUNCTION OF INTERSTATE 44 AND INTERSTATE 270

Like the Jewel Box in Forest Park, the Shaw Arboretum is a product of St. Louis's smoke-choked atmosphere in the 1920s. Coal smog was so horrible that administrators at the Missouri Botanical Garden established the arboretum in 1925, almost forty miles from the city, with the plan to move the living collections in their entirety to this new spot. Although the orchid collection (which has since been returned) made the pilgrimage, city ordinances were put in place that effectively began the clean-up process and the garden stayed in the city. The city retained the arboretum, however, as opportunity to cultivate a native Ozarkian landscape—particularly native pines and swamp plants of the border region between the Mississippi Valley and the mountains of the Ozarks farther west. A major feature for garden lovers is the five-acre wildflower garden.

Unlike most naturalistic gardens that are planted as a heterogeneous mixture, this bears the scientific stamp of its designers and is arranged according to plant communities: limestone glade, pine savanna, prairie, woodland, and wetland. The *Pinetum* at Shaw is world-renowned for its botanical selection as well as its beauty. The arrangements cover an extensive 55-acre landscape of meadows and woodlands. Ecological restoration has become a major focus at the arboretum in recent years. A major effort has been underway to eradicate exotic invasives and re-create the woodlands, meadows, and swamps that existed at the time of European contact. Considering that the arboretum encompasses 2,400 acres and 15 miles of walking trails, the transformation will be significant. The manor house on the property, dating to 1879, has been restored as a visitors center and a museum that exhibits the history of Missouri flora and the impact of humans on the land over 12,000 years.

BELOW: *An eclectic mix of color and texture pervade the Chance Garden.*

II Centralia: Chance Gardens

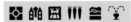

LOCATION: CORNER OF SNEED AND BRADFORD STREETS, TWENTY MILES NORTH OF COLUMBIA

Like many men of wealth in his day Albert Bishop Chance set out in his 30s for the Grand Tour abroad. He returned with an appreciation for cultivated European and Asian gardens, specifically Chinese gardens. On his return he hired landscape architect Maude Taylor Dawson to design his own private gardens. From the beginning he envisioned it as a philanthropic project, which he might someday be able to share this newfound treasure with the citizens of Centralia.

The small garden is filled with a variety of experiences. Following a meandering oval path from the back of the house (now a museum documenting the rise of the Chance

GARDEN OPEN: Dawn to dusk daily. ADMISSION: free.

FURTHER INFORMATION FROM: 319 East Sneed Street, Centralia 65240 (573) 682-5513

NEARBY SIGHTS OF INTEREST: American Horse Saddle Museum, Union Covered Bridge

Company) we proceed to an informally planted annual garden, in contrast to most gardens of this type. The low-lying, sun-filled beds are filled with an intermingling of flowers. The result is less embroidery than batik, a flowing in and out of color in haphazard but intriguing ways. Next the path passes over a small stream that bisects to the garden. Along its length is a garden of oriental influence, employing a layer of ever-greens and stone features, set beside a watercourse filled with koi. The path weaves around a rock grotto, the central feature, patterned on examples that Chance saw on his Asian travels, which also reference the limestone caves that are plentiful in Missouri. While in most Eastern traditions these functions are kept separated, Chance's oriental gardens are meant for both viewing and strolling through. The path allows visitors to walk through the displays, while Maude Taylor Dawson used design techniques to create a viewing garden, such as a foreshortening of space and layering of textures.

The Chance Gardens are well maintained by a local garden club. A recent addition of a rose garden has expanded the very personal vision of Chance (and his designer, Taylor), enabling the garden to be more relevant to a wider audience.

GARDEN OPEN: 9 am to 6 pm daily, April–October; 9 am to 5 pm, November–March.
ADMISSION: $5 adults, $4 seniors, $2 children 5–12 years.

FURTHER INFORMATION FROM: 1609 N.W. U.S. Highway 50, Kingsville 64061 (816) 697-2600

NEARBY SIGHTS OF INTEREST: James Reed Wildlife Refuge

12 Kingsville: Powell Gardens

LOCATION: HIGHWAY 50, BETWEEN HIGHWAY W AND HIGHWAY 131, FORTY MILES EAST OF KANSAS CITY

Although he made his fortune in business, George E. Powell always retained a strong connection to the farmland of his youth; in 1948 he purchased these 800 acres on the outskirts of Kansas City, then a family-run dairy farm. When the business failed, Powell donated the property to the Boy Scouts. And when that failed, he bought it back, and in the 1980s it was developed into a public garden, with support from the University of Missouri. Designed by Environmental Planning and Design of Pittsburgh, a national botanical garden design firm, the garden's central feature is a twelve -acre lake that forms a backbone for the horticultural displays. The perennial gardens, featuring over 500 varieties arranged along strolling paths in a flowing, free-form style and organized into twelve theme gardens. At the center of this space is a rock and water-fall garden, featuring two cascading streams and several quiet nooks for passive, contemplative interaction with the garden. Following the major path further around the lake we come to a wildflower meadow, containing a maturing selection of native and non-native plants set into a hillside over the lake. In the early years of the garden, Marjorie Powell Allen hired Arkansas architect Fay Jones to design several structures in the garden, including a magnificently arched, wooden-beamed chapel. Jones, who was influenced by Frank Lloyd Wright yet possessed a more mystical sense of nature, emphasized the subliminal interplay between the airy structure and the surrounding meadow and woodland. Jones' firm, Fay Jones and Maurice Jennings, designed the visitor center and small conservatory.

Sensitive design and natural splendor define the Powell Gardens.

1   NORTH DAKOTA

2   SOUTH DAKOTA

   NEBRASKA

OGALLALA   GRAND ISLAND   4   3   OMAHA

LINCOLN

5

   KANSAS   TOPEKA   7

DODGE CITY   6   WICHITA

8   TULSA

9   OKLAHOMA CITY

10

11   OKLAHOMA

1 Dunseith: International Peace Garden	6 Wichita: Botanica, The Wichita Gardens
2 Brookings: McCrory Gardens	7 Overland Park: Overland Park Arboretum
3 Omaha: Omaha Botanical Gardens	and Botanical Garden
4 Lincoln: Sunken Garden	
5 Lincoln: University of Nebraska, Lincoln	
Botanical Gardens	

8   Tulsa: Philbrook Gardens
9   Oklahoma City: Myriad Botanical Gardens
10   Oklahoma City: Cowboy Hall of Fame
11   Stillwater: Oklahoma Botanical Garden and
Arboretum

GREAT PLAINS:

North Dakota, South Dakota, Nebraska, Kansas, Oklahoma

I t might seem odd to group together five large states. What can North Dakota possibly have in common with Oklahoma? The same can be asked about Nebraska and Kansas. The short answer is both "a lot" and "a little." We pass a geographic (and political) border when we venture west from Minnesota, Iowa, and Missouri. Something happens. The land and climate change, and so do characteristics of people and culture. The change is subtle, and perhaps not always noticeable, yet through the lens of garden design the differences are very clear.

As a rule, gardens are relatively larger in the Great Plains than in the eastern Midwest states. This makes sense given the greater geography. Yet there are fewer municipalities and institutions willing and able to develop a new garden. Thus, it comes as no surprise that universities play a major role in the garden culture of this region. In Oklahoma, Oklahoma State University underwrites the plentiful gardens of the Arboretum in Stillwater. South Dakota's only public garden is located on the campus of South Dakota State. And Nebraska features two university-oriented institutions. While horticultural research is important at each of these gardens, the universities also see public education as a part of their mission, and at each you will find home demonstration gardens that exhibit practical uses for shrubs, maintaining flower gardens, and general care of the typical domestic landscape.

There are also some exciting and unusual gardens in this region as well. The Myriad Botanical Garden in Oklahoma City occupies one of the most unusual conservatories in the country, even while it houses a fairly conventional collection.

OPPOSITE: *Thousands of brilliantly colored annuals beautify Botanica, The Wichita Gardens*

Designed by Conklin Rossant, the conservatory structure is perfectly cylindrical, which creates a spacious, vaulted interior space for plants. Hundreds of miles north, on the North Dakotan border with Canada, is another notable garden. The International Peace Garden was conceived as a gesture between Canada and the U.S. to symbolize the friendship between the two countries. Marked by two striking modernist towers, the garden actually spans the border and features a transnational chapel where congregations from each side hold services.

Oklahoma may geographically (and culturally) be closer to Texas of the South than the Great Plains of the Midwest. But its gardens define Oklahoma as a midwestern place. The Philbrook Museum in Tulsa is a country place estate that would be as much at home in Ohio or Michigan. The arboretum in Stillwater,

A vista seamlessly travels through formal and informal gardens at Philbrook.

Oklahoma, makes clear the demarcation between east and west; what we find here—and indeed all the way up through the region—are the last gasps of a climate and way of life (or gardening) before it heads for mountains.

Dunseith:
International Peace Garden

LOCATION: ON THE U.S.-CANADIAN BORDER, FIFTEEN MILES NORTH OF
DUNSEITH, IN THE TURTLE HILLS

GARDEN OPEN: Dawn to dusk
daily, mid-May–mid-
September. **ADMISSION:** free.

FURTHER INFORMATION FROM:
RR, Box 116, Dunseith 58329
(701) 263-4390
www.peacegarden.com

NEARBY SIGHTS OF INTEREST:
Turtle Mountain Chippewa
Heritage Center (U.S.),
Badger Creek Museum
(Manitoba, Canada)

Dr. Henry Moore, a Canadian horticulturist, hatched the idea of a botanical garden spanning the border between the United States and Canada on his way home from a gardeners association meeting in the U. S. in 1928. Wouldn't it be great, Moore thought, to use a garden, with all its symbolism and connection to nature, to represent the lasting peace between the two countries. After a brief selection period, Moore, with the backing of constituents in both countries, selected this old farmland in the middle of North Dakota, in part because it is located near the geographic center of the border. The garden actually spans the border, and while visitors are allowed to enter it freely from both sides, everyone must pass through international customs upon leaving. (A driver's license is required for Canadian and U. S. citizens; foreign nationals must show a passport.)

Horticulturally, the garden is a showcase for an ornate display of bedded-out annuals. A major attraction is a floral clock planted into the side of a small mound. The stainless steel hands actually rotate around the face of begonias, cannas, and other bright flowers. In the center of the garden, spanning the two countries, is a chapel that hosts denominations from Dunseith to the south and the Canadian town of Bossevain to the north. Balancing this unobtrusive structure on the other side of a grass circle are two enormous H-shaped towers, which

A verdant and vibrant landscape links Canada and the U.S. at the International Peace Garden.

a field of sunflowers engulfs at their base. From here extends a relatively flat spine, cut through by a small creek planted with riparian perennials and hardy shrubs. As it runs through the center of an open, grassy expanse, it bisects two triangular gardens of annuals that are ritually planted in the pattern of each country's flag. A large oval pond, surrounded by an abundant floral groundplane, culminates this central axis and the garden as whole. The garden continues to promote the peaceful interrelationship between Canada and the U.S., not only through the symbolic gesture of the gardens but through the literal expression of its inspirational literature. An onsite museum features an exhibit on the Civilian Conservation Corps (CCC), which built the lodge and many of the stone picnic sites in the garden at the height of the depression.

GARDEN OPEN: Dawn to dusk daily. ADMISSION: free.

FURTHER INFORMATION FROM: Horticulture, Forest, Landscape, and Parks Dept., SDSU, Brookings 57007-0996 (605) 688-5136

NEARBY SIGHTS OF INTEREST: Little Town on the Prairie, Bramble Park Zoo

2 Brookings: McCrory Gardens

LOCATION: CORNER OF 6TH STREET AND 22ND AVENUE, DOWNTOWN BROOKINGS, FIFTY MILES NORTH OF SIOUX FALLS

"Beauty is its own excuse for being," so states the McCrory Gardens tour pamphlet. While striving for the beautiful, these gardens have also been cultivated over 35 years to be an educational resource for South Dakota residents. South Dakota State University, which owns the gardens, is a land grant college that is committed to its mission of public education. In 1966 the horticulture department began work on a modest flower garden to commemorate professor S. A. McCrory, a former department chair. This first garden, quite formal in its design, had a large central area cut by transverse axes to create a well balanced structure for annuals, perennials, and assorted groundcovers, all of which are hardy species, if not native to eastern South Dakota. This traditional approach has informed the development of the garden at large, which today covers about 20 acres, with an arboretum encompassing another 45 acres. The gardens are divided into specialty plant areas such as irises or hostas, theme gardens such as white garden and a blue garden, and educational areas such as a collection of plants used in medicine. The university uses the garden to conduct research on turf grasses and other plants, yet its overall focus remains on creating well-designed, beautiful gardens. A major attraction are the two *All-America Display* judging gardens in which plant experts from around the country monitor and judge herbaceous plants. Each year the university seems to outdo itself with the best that botanical science has to offer, packed into these large rectangular beds. Elsewhere the gardens are quieter, more reflective. An overlarge rose garden, occupying the north end of the garden, literally spills over with foliage into the elliptical path and central circle of paving that defines it. Nearby the *Great Lawn* provides a visual contrast with an encircling border of peonies, daylilies, and hardy northern shrubs, such as Ruckmore arborvitae and Homestead buckeye. A new maze garden, constructed in Nugget ninebark (*Physocarpus opulifolius*), was installed in 1995. To address the growing interest in environmental gardening, such as using natives to decrease water consumption and the need for fertilizers, the university has invested in its arboretum, which showcases many native tree species. Yet the gardens remain quite traditional, looking more toward the 1950s than the 2000s, a refreshing stance in a world of continual change.

3 Omaha: Omaha Botanical Gardens

LOCATION: CORNER OF **6**TH AND CEDAR STREETS, BETWEEN THE OLD MARKET AND THE HENRY ZOO, NEAR THE MISSOURI RIVER

GARDEN OPEN: 9 am to 4 pm daily; closed Monday.
ADMISSION: free.

Omaha's botanical garden was the dream of local newspaper garden columnist Helena Street, who first proposed the idea in 1982. Street gathered together a group of knowledgeable and dedicated gardeners to create a board of directors, and in 1993 the garden was born. The directors and Street, now in her nineties and involved in everyday activities, design the master plan and individual gardens. The botanical garden is still building-out the 150-acre site, yet the garden already contains a full rose garden, shade garden, herb garden, and children's garden. The most recent addition is a small arboretum and bird sanctuary. Until the trees grow large enough to provide natural habitat, feeding stations and bird houses are provided to attract birds. A low boardwalk extends into a marshy area, where a viewing pavilion will be built. Also on the horizon is a new English walled garden, which should be planted in the spring of 2000. Among the existing garden areas, the shade garden is the most established, perhaps because of the large canopy of trees that hang over the property's fence line and provide the cooling setting. A pathway weaves between assemblages of hostas and ferns, which are interplanted with hyacinths and annuals to give the area color. The rose garden is also fully developed, designed on a gridded scheme with over 2,000 bushes. The children's garden with a new bird sanctuary provides hands-on gardening experiences for kids.

FURTHER INFORMATION FROM:
P.O. Box 24089,
Omaha 68124
(402) 346-4002

NEARBY SIGHTS OF INTEREST:
Henry Doorly Zoo, Western Heritage Center

Lincoln: Sunken Gardens

GARDEN OPEN: dawn to dusk daily. **ADMISSION:** free.

FURTHER INFORMATION FROM: 2740 A Street, Lincoln 68502 402-441-7847

NEARBY SIGHTS OF INTEREST: Children's Zoo

LOCATION: 27TH STREET AND D STREET, SOUTH OF INTERSTATE 80, NEAR THE CHILDREN'S ZOO

Lincoln's Sunken Gardens were designed and built in 1931, at the height of the Depression. It was as much a beautification scheme for the city, aimed at raising spirits, as it was a means of engaging a restless population of unemployed men. Over 200 souls were hired, and no one could work more than two, eight-hour shifts in a week. Everyone was paid $6.40. With such meager compensation this intrepid army transformed an old watercourse, which for many years had deteriorated into an unofficial city dumping ground, into a one-and-a-half-acre paradise in the middle of Lincoln.

The garden itself was designed by the city's floriculturist Fred Goebel and his son Henry. The dominant feature was rock, of which they imported several tons from the surrounding county. Stitched into the white limestone retaining walls was a carpet of perennial sedum. Against this canvas the Goebels planted a wildly colorful flower garden. In the center of the garden is a four-step waterfall, cut from limestone. The naturalistic design is accentuated by a backdrop of blue verbena and the purplish hints of fountain grass (*Pennisetum setaceum*) to give this focal point to the garden a sharp, icy aspect. In the lower areas, on the east and north sides, are borders of various perennials and annuals, mixed together in large bands of color. There is an attempt to be orderly here, but not overly formal. A handsome gravel walking path passes along the length of the display, slowly allowing the senses to relish in the abundance of

A classic Victorian mode underlies Lincoln's Sunken Gardens.

flowers. In the middle of the garden are two reflecting pools filled with brilliantly hued koi and water lilies. According to city records the first lilies purchased in the 1930s came from the Missouri Botanical Garden and were among the first tropicals used in a midwestern garden.

Lining the western side, along the ledges behind the waterfall, are *viewing gardens* that mix sedum and rock combinations with a variety of flowers. There is also an *herb garden, shade garden,* and Victorian *"wheel garden"* of daffodils and Rudbeckia. Across the street from the Sunken Gardens is the *Antelope Rose Garden,* so named for the river that once ran through this section of town and carved these depressions into the landscape. The garden is an All-America Rose Society display garden and is designed as a circle, with a central axis of hedge and annuals. Originally planted in 1970 and restored in 1992, it features the full range of grandifloras, hybrid teas, miniatures, and foribundas.

5 Lincoln: University of Nebraska Lincoln Botanical Gardens

LOCATION: 10TH STREET AND VINE STREET (CITY CAMPUS); 33RD STREET AND HOLDREGE STREET (EAST CAMPUS)

GARDEN OPEN: Dawn to dusk daily. ADMISSION: free.

When the University of Nebraska Lincoln (UNL) was founded in 1869 one important focus was agricultural experimentation. To this end, the founders created a separate campus for farming studies, which at that time was outside the city limits. Among the test plots where students and professors engaged in wide-ranging research, from developing pesticides to raising disease resistant hogs, several garden-minded people began planting lovely landscape features. The oldest remnant is the entrance mall, constructed in 1910 when a trolley was built along Holdrege Street. Designed by landscape gardener W. H. Dunman, the mall features an allée of venerable oaks, currently underplanted with a variety of showy flowers and groundcover. Across the street is a curious tribute to the first superintendent of the agricultural college, S. W. Perin: a replica of his porch planted around by historic varieties, including fruit trees and spring bulbs. Nearby is a collection of old roses, which though unruly in their growth patterns provide a lovely perfume. Deeper within the campus is an iris garden and a small, five-acre arboretum of hostas, viburnum, and mature canopy trees that date back to the early twentieth century.

The main city campus of the university is located a short distance from here and features several botanical gardens stitched into the grounds. Chief among these is the *Cather*

FURTHER INFORMATION FROM: 1340 North 17th Street, Lincoln 68588-0609 (402) 472-2679

NEARBY SIGHTS OF INTEREST: Children's Zoo, State Historical Society Museum

Classical columns and abundant tulips deepen the mood.

Garden, a small prairie garden. Instead of trying to express the natural expansiveness of the prairie landscape, this garden is given an urban touch. Flowers are arranged according to bloom to create a seasonal rhythm of color. Included are columbine and Joe Pye weed, as well as native sumac and purple coneflower, to give the space a varied, textural appearance as well as ample color. The garden is named in honor of the novelist Willa Cather, who grew up in Nebraska and attended the University of Nebraska. There are several formal gardens on the city campus, including border gardens that frame the entrance to the library and a sculpture garden containing works by contemporary artists.

GARDEN OPEN: 9 am to 5 pm Monday–Saturday, 1 pm to 5 pm Sunday, April–December; 9 am to 5 pm Monday–Friday January–March. **ADMISSION:** $4.50 adults, $4.00 seniors, $2.00 students, free children under 6 years.

FURTHER INFORMATION FROM: 701 North Amidon, Wichita 67203 (316) 264-0448 www.botanica.org

NEARBY SIGHTS OF INTEREST: Vietnam War Memorial

6 Wichita: Botanica, The Wichita Gardens

LOCATION: CORNER OF MURDOCK AND AMIDON, IN SIM PARK, NEAR THE RIVER AND MUSEUMS

The Wichita Gardens claim that they may "possibly be the most beautiful spot anywhere in the Great Plains." Perhaps a boastful statement, but any trip to Wichita ought to include a stopover here. The gardens subsist on the energy and goodwill of local residents and philanthropists, and although they are eclectic each individual area is beautifully maintained and well-designed. Visitors are greeted by an entry garden that is redesigned every few months with a new display of flowering plants laid against a backdrop of old, stately canopy trees. Within the garden proper, must-see areas include the *Aquatic Collection* that is arranged within a naturalistic pond. The giant water platter in the center of the water is an extraordinary specimen, with leaves that grow to a diameter of seven feet. One precinct of the garden is given over to more formal designs, including a modest radial *rose garden*. Along the flat edge sits a scalloped fountain, illuminated at night, and encircled by thousands of brilliantly colored annuals. A semicircle of peonies balances the composition.

There are several more utilitarian garden spaces at Botanica, including a teaching garden and a *Xeriscape* garden, which displays water conservation principles. Botanica also includes several naturalistic gardens, including a meadow, a woodland glade, and a pinetum.

BELOW: Framed vistas help to shape the experience of the garden.

7 Overland Park: Overland Park Arboretum and Botanical Garden

LOCATION: CORNER OF 179TH STREET AND ANTIOCH AVENUE, THREE-QUARTERS-MILE WEST OF HIGHWAY 69, FIFTEEN MILES SOUTHWEST OF KANSAS CITY

GARDEN OPEN: 7 am to 8 pm daily, mid-April–mid-October; 7 am to 5 pm mid-October– mid-April. ADMISSION: free.

FURTHER INFORMATION FROM: 8500 Santa Fe, Overland Park 66212
(913) 685-3604

NEARBY SIGHTS OF INTEREST: Mahaffie Farmstead

Most arable land around Kansas City was converted into farmland years ago. That unmistakable truth has meant that public and private interests have left land that was unsuitable for agriculture—either because of poor soil, poor drainage, or both— to go wild or to develop it. The Overland Park Arboretum and Botanical Garden occupies one of these forgotten sites, a 300-acre tract that descends toward Wolf Creek, itself a tributary of the Missouri River. The garden, which was only begun in earnest four years ago, is intended to foster native plant species. To this end, work has already begun on managing the woodlands on-site so that intrusive species like honey locusts and cedars are reduced in favor of the ash, oak, hornbeam, and hickory that have grown here for millennia. Several gardens are newly built or in development. The most established is the *water garden*, which features a large manmade pond and stream with a waterfall. The plant material includes a medley of milkweed and budleia, both of which provide nectar for a profusion of butterflies. Literally, the director of the garden quips, the collection is "moth eaten."

A recent addition to the garden is a woodland area with a dense *fern garden*, cut through by a flagstone walk. There is also a *pawpaw walk* and a *rhododendron hill*. Another newcomer will be the *Legacy*

Garden, a collection of old time plants, such as heritage roses. Also new will be the *Discovery Garden,* including a children's area and historical tree path, with donated trees from the Mount Vernon estate in Virginia.

Wildflowers run through the entire arboretum, filling it with bloom in the spring. Varieties include prickly pear, coneflower, bellflower, and dogtooth violet, a small flower with a quick bloom. For what the gardens lack in presence they make up for in enthusiasm, with a staff committed to implementing a twenty-year plan. Thanks to the region's favorable summer climate in recent years, these young gardens have filled out beautifully. Much is expected for the future.

8 Tulsa: Philbrook Gardens

GARDEN OPEN: Dawn to dusk daily. **ADMISSION:** free.
MUSEUM OPEN: 10 am to 5 pm Tuesday–Saturday; 10 am to 8 pm Thursday, 11 am to 5 pm Sunday. **ADMISSION:** $5 adults, $3 seniors and students, free children 12 years and under.

FURTHER INFORMATION FROM:
2727 South Rockford Road, Tulsa 74114
(918) 749-7941
www.philbrook.org

NEARBY SIGHTS OF INTEREST:
Fenster Museum of Jewish Art

LOCATION: 27TH STREET AND PEORIA AVENUE, MIDTOWN TULSA, NEAR UTICA SQUARE SHOPPING CENTER

For a half-century, landscape architects Hare and Hare of Kansas City, Missouri, gave form to the formless Central Plains, including the design of the Waite Phillips estate in Tulsa, known today as Philbrook. Phillips, an oil magnate, built the Italianate villa in 1926, to a design by architect Edward B. Delk. The Hares took their cues from the magisterial aspect of the manor, and designed the landscape with both formal, Italian-inspired terraces near the house and more informal, English-inspired landscapes farther away. From a stone terrace near the house the eye takes a textbook journey down a perfect axis and across a *parterre garden.* The terrace itself is adorned with potted plants and several shell-shaped bowls, through which water flows and then links into a rill system and descends down into the parterre garden. This area, which slopes down toward the woods, features crisscrossing paths and a system of triangular beds, planted with turf grass. The land begins to ramp up again in the dramatic *rock garden,* constructed in limestone and featuring a petrified stump as its centerpiece. This area has been recently restored. Downslope, following the water that provides a link through the formal gardens, lies a reflecting pool at the edge of the informal landscape, designed by Hare and Hare in an English style of rolling topography and specimen trees. The pool is surrounded by banks of bulbs, herbaceous shrubs, and tropical standards (plants trained into trees), such as hibiscus and lantana, which mature instantly during the summer. On sunny days the house is reflected in the pool. A wall of 80-year-old magnolias mask these formal areas from the pleasure grounds below. A few years ago landscape architect Joe Howell developed a plan to create a new formal garden on the south side of the house (annual around a central fountain), an idea originally expressed in the earlier plans by Hare and Hare.

The house is open to the public as a museum of decorative and visual arts. The gardens inspire exhibits of landscape painting and are studied as works of art.

Transverse orientations help to connect spaces.

🗄 🍽 ♀ ⚘ ⚱

GARDEN OPEN: 6 am to 11 pm
daily. **ADMISSION:** $4 adults,
$3 seniors and students 13–18
years, $2 children under 13
years.

FURTHER INFORMATION FROM:
100 Myriad Gardens,
Oklahoma City 73102
(405) 297-3995

NEARBY SIGHTS OF INTEREST:
Oklahoma City Art Museum,
Overholser Mansion

*A cylindrical conservatory
provides a whole new way of
experiencing a collection of
tropicals.*

9 Oklahoma City: Myriad Botanical Gardens

LOCATION: RENO AND ROBINSON AVENUES, IN THE HEART OF DOWNTOWN

In the 1960s Oklahoma City hired international architect I. M. Pei to create a master plan for the future of this small plains metropolis. The jewel in Pei's scheme was a large botanical garden, fashioned after Tivoli Gardens in Copenhagen. The Myriad Botanical Gardens came to fruition over 20 years later. The anchor of the gardens is the *Crystal Bridge Conservatory*, a striking glass tube designed by the firm Conklin Rossant of New York City. The structure is suspended by an immense system of interior trusses that intermingle with the maturing palms to create a dazzling mid-air display. The conservatory is broken down into three climatic zones—dry mountain tropicals (also called Mediterranean plants), semi-arid (American and African desert plants), and rain forest. The palms first capture the eye, followed by a plethora of bromeliads, staghorn ferns, and ancient cycads. A system of ramps and tunnels in this vertical space create the sense that the building is filled with things to see in these botanical surroundings.

The seventeen acres of rolling terrain outside the conservatory contain an array of different gardens, set up both with an

educational intent and as one of Oklahoma's finer public spaces. Adjacent to the conservatory the curators create yearly displays of annuals. Stepping down from here, by way of a few terraces, the landscape opens to a large lake, around which a number of excellent garden areas are arranged as an informal walk. A recent addition is the *Hosta Garden*, in which several dozen varieties sporting variously colored and spotted leaf arrangements have been planted along the lakeshore, in a shady area. The landscape has a subtle Japanese feel, in that it dips in and out of a contrived hillside, affording short glimpses of the surrounding area before leading the eye back into small nodes or nooks. The conservatory remains constant, a dominant feature on the horizon and an important connection back to the city, reminding us that this is an urban garden.

10 Oklahoma City: Cowboy Hall of Fame

LOCATION: OFF INTERSTATES 35 AND 44, NORTHEAST OF DOWNTOWN

GARDEN OPEN: 8 am to 6 pm daily, April–September; 9 am to 5 pm daily, October–March.
ADMISSION: free.

LOCATION:
1700 NE 63rd Street,
Oklahoma City 73111
(405) 478-2250
www.cowboyhalloffame.org

NEARBY SIGHTS OF INTEREST:
National Softball Hall of Fame, Oklahoma City Zoo

The Cowboy Hall of fame, true to its calling, has assembled one of the largest collections of cowboy arcana this side of Death Valley. The museum is located on Persimmon Hill, just outside of town, and is planted round with several flower gardens. The entrance is marked by the sculpture *Sundown,* which sits in a circle of purple fountain grass, lantanas, and zinnias, which make the statement loud and clear that, indeed, we have arrived. Behind the museum, the landscape opens up into two different gardens. The *Southerland Gardens,* named for a local garden enthusiast, features native perennials such as love grass, little blue stem, coneflowers, and Black-eyed Susans, many of which the curator has dug up from her pasture. Arranged along a path, the beds are young, but with a couple of very good years under their belt, defy their age. The walkway culminates in a rock garden with running stream stocked with catfish and bass, and planted in waterlilies.

The *Hambrick Gardens,* located farther along, reflect the plains landscape: a collection of post oaks, pin oaks, and fescue grasses form a natural backdrop to cowboy art, including an overly large statue of Buffalo Bill. There are several plaques nestled in the long plains grasses commemorating famous bulls of the rodeo circuit.

GARDEN OPEN: Dawn to dusk daily. **ADMISSION:** free.

FURTHER INFORMATION FROM:
3425 West Virginia Avenue,
Stillwater 74074
(405) 744-6460
www.hortla.okstate.edu

NEARBY SIGHTS OF INTEREST:
Cherokee Strip Museum, Jim
Thorpe Home

II Stillwater: Oklahoma Botanical Garden and Arboretum

LOCATION: NEAR THE CORNER OF SANGER ROAD AND HIGHWAY 51, SIXTY MILES NORTHEAST OF OKLAHOMA CITY

Interstate 35 is a geographical divide across the state of Oklahoma. To the east lies rolling, verdant landscape of farmlands and rich soil. The bottoms of rivers are green with forest. To the west, the land stretches out towards arid plains. Texas is not too far, both spatially and philosophically. But this border land is interesting, and where we find the Oklahoma Botanical Garden and Arboretum, we see the last traces of eastern/midwestern cultures in a head-on encounter with the West.

Most of this 100-acre garden is given over to an arboretum of Oklahoma native trees and cleared meadows—the final stretch of such landscape before it turns to flat, treeless plains. In the center of the collection is the *Studio Garden,* where a local gardening television show is filmed. Sited within this three-acre garden are a number of specialty and ever-changing theme gardens. Of the latter, provocative ideas sometimes rule, such as a recent *Junk Garden,* which used old tires and broken bottles as the architectural structuring for an array of flowers. Color themes and historical traditions also hold sway. Permanent garden rooms include a water garden, bedded annuals, a perennial border garden, herb garden, a Japanese garden, and a rock garden. Museum-like in its composition, a small railway winds through the site tying it all together. A children's garden has recently joined the mix. It features a concrete terrace in the shape of the state of Oklahoma, with rocks depicting various towns and cities. Classes from local schools are frequently to be found here learning about the local flora and fauna.

Although the garden and arboretum are associated with the Oklahoma State University department of horticulture and landscape architecture, the gardens are the work of a grounds manager, who develops the several theme gardens each year.

At the junction of geographies, the Oklahoma Botanical Garden looks both east and west.

Biographies

DOWNING, ANDREW JACKSON (1815–1852) After Thomas Jefferson, the father of American landscape architecture whose *Treatise on Landscape Gardening and Rural Architecture* influenced American tastes for half a century.

HARE AND HARE COMPANY Based in Kansas City, Missouri, this landscape company was founded by Herbert S. and Sidney Hare, father and son. In addition to various colleges and parks in the Midwest and Great Plains, they designed the Philbrook Estate in Tulsa, Oklahoma.

JEKYLL [pronounced JEE'kul], **GERTRUDE** (1842–1932) Artist and garden designer famous for developing the English "cottage garden style," notable for its informal and impressionistic use of color laid against a geometric background.

JENSEN, JENS (1860–1951) Chicago landscape architect whose "prairie style" transformed gardening in the Midwest. Jensen also founded the Clearing, a "school of the soil" in Green Bay, Wisconsin.

MANNING, WARREN (1860–1938) Landscape architect of Stan Hywet Hall in Akron, Ohio. Early in his career Manning served as a draftsman in the office of Frederick Law Olmsted, helping to design the Biltmore Estate in Asheville, North Carolina, and later helped to found the landscape architecture school at Harvard University.

OLMSTED BROTHERS A Boston-based landscape company founded by Frederick Law Olmsted (1822–1903), designer of Central Park in New York City. Under his son and nephew, the company continued to design estate gardens, parks, and campus master plans well into the twentieth century

SIMONDS, JOHN O. Son of O. C. Simonds, a landscape architect who designed in the prairie style. Responsible for the Chicago Botanic Garden, among others.

SIMONDS, OSSIAN COLE (O. C.) (1857–1931) One of the leaders of the prairie style of landscape architecture, and a designer of several estates and gardens throughout the Midwest.

Glossary

exedra (Greek) A semicircular outdoor bench with an unusually high back; in ancient Greece and Rome, used as a meeting place.

riparian Refers to plants or plant communities that grow on the edges or banks of rivers or lakes.

Shakespearean garden A garden composed of herbs and flowers mentioned in the works of Shakespeare.

tufa A type of rock that stabilizes acidic soils, with sharp edges and a porous composition; frequently used in the design of pools and ponds.

Index

Acknowledgments

Books always take far more time and energy than expected. I'd like to thank my wife, Lani (to whom this book is dedicated), and my parents (Gary and Frankie Bennett) and in-laws (Barry and Marilyn Bevacqua) for their help and support. Also, applause for Bruce and Julia and Hadj and Kim for use of their guest rooms during my quest. As usual, my editor Jan Cigliano has been friend, advisor, and trusted guide.

Photograph credits

iii, 29: Luke Messinger
4:Jim Juster
6, 7:Richard Hirneisen
6–9:Cranbrook
8:Thomas Treuter
12:Frank Telewski
20, 23:Stan Hywet Hall
21 H. K. Barnett

22 Barb Schlueter
32 Photo Arts Club
37:Carl Wernte
43, 45–46, 48:Paul Bennett
78, 80:Buettner and Associates
84:Greg Helgeson
102–05:Jack Jennings
122:Alan Storjohann